THE CHURCH'S PART IN EDUCATION
1833–1941

THE CHURCH'S PART IN EDUCATION · 1833-1941

WITH SPECIAL REFERENCE TO THE WORK OF THE NATIONAL SOCIETY

BY

C. K. FRANCIS BROWN

" In England popular education originated with no statesman, and was nurtured for no political end. It sprang from the action of the Church and the philanthropy of individuals."

Mr. Cowper-Temple in the House of Commons, Feb. 18th, 1857.

LONDON

NATIONAL SOCIETY
69 GREAT PETER STREET,
WESTMINSTER, S.W. I

SOCIETY FOR PROMOTING
CHRISTIAN KNOWLEDGE
NORTHUMBERLAND AVENUE, W.C. 2

1942

MADE IN GREAT BRITAIN

AUTHOR'S NOTE

IT is with real pleasure that one acknowledges a few of the many kindnesses received while this book was being written. Most of the text of an Oxford B.Litt. thesis is embodied therein.

My chief obligation is to Mr. H. E. M. Icely, Reader in Education in the University of Oxford, whose vast knowledge of English schools and of comparative education was unreservedly mine to draw upon.

Dr. Basil Yeaxlee gave one an insight into the Nonconformist point of view.

Miss Shuckburgh, Librarian of the Board of Education, went out of her way to be helpful, as did the Rev. Dr. F. L. Cross of Pusey House, Oxford. Mr. E. R. J. Hussey, C.M.G., Secretary of the National Society, placed the Society's archives at one's disposal at all hours and Miss Shotter has always been most helpful in her guidance as to their use.

In various ways my friend, Mr. Maurice Reckitt, the Rev. V. J. K. Brook, Fellow of All Souls and Censor of St. Catherine's, and the Harold Buxton trustees helped to make this book possible.

C.K.F.B.

June, 1941.

CONTENTS

HISTORICAL INTRODUCTION TO 1833

As a symbol of England the oak is singularly expressive of many characteristics of our native land. It is tiny and insignificant as a seedling, it grows for the most part in the face of every disadvantage and lack of encouragement, while for decades it gives little promise of its massive maturity. If, again, we study the full-grown giant with the historian's eye we find the tree's history stretching back into the distant past, its origins obscured by fancy and legend. It is gnarled and twisted in part by age, but more as the result of holding its own with the varied influences of storm and tempest, and the more subtle enmity of frost. Its timber may show deep fissures, yet in its power to resist stresses and strains it has no equal. In the study of national institutions such as our ancient universities or Parliament or the English legal system the same qualities of sturdy independence are seen, a certain lack of definition and a tendency for an institution to remain unrecognized until fairly established.

In the administrative sense, we have never had a planned and co-ordinated educational system until modern times. St. Augustine of Canterbury [1] in the seventh century may be regarded as the father of English education, but the cultural and intellectual needs of the English people have never been systematically catered for on the same scale as their spiritual needs, for example, were met by the formation of parishes and dioceses ascribed to Theodore of Tarsus. " The educational system of this country is not logical, nor has it symmetry : it has not been thought out by legislators or statesmen, and imposed from above upon the nation. At the same time it is not haphazard, but it has grown from practical needs, and is now indissolubly bound up with the national life. It cannot be understood apart from the national history, for it is the product of the national character. One striking feature of that character is its capacity for making an illogical compromise work in practice, and for getting things done without bothering overmuch about theory. We are tolerant of anomalies, and patient with survivals, so long as they produce results that are worth while. The history of our education is full of instances of this genius for action and indifference

I

to theory, which lead our critics to belittle our thinking powers and to represent us as a nation intimidated in the presence of a new idea. But in practice we have produced schools which are more powerful for the formation of character, which awake greater and more permanent loyalties, which provide greater scope for individual effort than those of any other people of the present or the past." [2]

Up to the time of the Reformation places of learning of many different kinds are found: cathedral,[3] monastic and nunnery schools; the palace schools of Alfred and the schools of courtesy for young nobles; parish primary schools taught by a " clerk "; grammar schools, including guild and chantry schools; the teaching of the friars; colleges proper like Winchester and Eton or the earlier Merton; the foundations in the two ancient universities and others that came near to being at Reading and Stamford and Northampton. The oral teaching of the clergy on the duties of the Christian life, the church's services, the representational arts found in every parish, even story and legend were all, although not generally reckoned a part of formal education, genuine educative forces helping the unlettered.

How did all these teaching institutions come into being? The answer is that they were set up as a result of papal and conciliar injunction with episcopal license and under episcopal inspection or through the promptings of individual conscience in response to local needs. " Charity " rather than a scheme of organized planning created this teaching work, in which " the state " took no part. Education was always directly in the hands of churchmen and it is absolutely true to say that the ethos, the philosophy of life, were invariably and in every sense in accord with the Catholic faith.

As it is, after all, essentially a spiritual matter the church was logically bound to exclude heterodoxy from education. After the Reformation the proportion of monastic property that went to endow education under Henry VIII was pitiably small, while the Edwardian suppression and confiscation of guilds, chantries and schools robbed the English people of a valuable part of their educational heritage. But the emergent state did not make new claims as against the church: in 1410 the King's Bench Division had disclaimed jurisdiction in matters of education as belonging to the spirituality and this disclaimer largely held good until the nineteenth century. Questions of related property raised different issues.

Throughout the years of Elizabeth the bishops as officials of the church settlement licensed the schoolmasters, Archbishop Laud did not relax the church's superintendence, and the position of those who were unable to conform worsened under the Clarendon code of the second Charles.

The long struggle for educational equality for those outside the establishment (and, incidentally, the Elizabethan conception of the unity of the *res publica*) may be said to have virtually ended only in 1870, but throughout the eighteenth century the dissenting Sunday schools, boarding schools and academies—which have much of the heroic in their history that belongs to pious minority movements—grew in numbers and importance. It is probably true to say that they worked fairly harmoniously, under most diocesans, alongside their anglican counterparts : certainly in their aloofness from the traditional they developed new characteristics that were later merged in the main stream to its enrichment. Men of all types of religious thought were beginning to see the necessity, for both sociological and religious reasons, of providing schools.

This century witnesses a surprising amount of effort on the part of both individuals and societies [4] to found parish, charity and other schools, the beginnings of the voluntary system in the nineteenth century. Especially is this true in the case of Wesley's work for education. The Sunday schools of Raikes, his predecessors [5] and successors, are an important new departure in this century of experiment in education.

In the absence of official pronouncements we can consider the attitude of the church to the problems of education in the first quarter of the nineteenth century only by inquiring into the ideals of parties or representative churchmen.

The distinction between high and low church was largely the distinction between the historic political parties on the question of authoritarianism as a principle. Real theological or sociological bases appeared later : high churchmen were tories and low churchmen were whigs. The former were wrapped in a sleepy orthodoxy, supported the war with France and were mainly concerned to act as bulwarks of stability, and the whigs do not show up any better as churchmen. The episcopal and archidiaconal " charges " of men of both parties were much concerned with the dissenters and evangelicals as dangerous and enthusiastic innovators. Neither party had any thought of the necessity of political or economic change

and adjustment: they did not understand the nature of the
organic disturbances taking place around them in society
through the Industrial revolution, with the social and intellectual awakening that came from France's own revolution.
The one bright patch is the work of the evangelicals, but their
good works sprang from a real zeal for souls born of a living
but untheological faith that had no formulated doctrine of
God, man and society. They lacked an intellectual dynamic
and were primarily pure individualists, leaving to others the
statement of the case for corporate action by the church as
a divine society. It is, perhaps, significant that the incredible
mass of ecclesiastical abuses—pluralism, non-residence, episcopal nepotism and so on—was attacked chiefly by non-
churchmen, for even the evangelicals were philanthropists
and not social reformers. The sense of property and privilege
took the place of that social responsibility which is the mainspring of concern for others, not least in the matter of educating the masses. The new ideas most vital were the result of
the French revolution as seen through the eyes of Burke rather
than the teaching of the Gospel: secularists rather than
churchmen had their eyes on the New Jerusalem.

We may now ask what the church was doing at this time
of her great wealth and influence for the children of the
country. Statistics in 1833 are positively medieval in their
unreliability, but the following figures [6] from the Government
census may be given for what they are worth.

1833. Children in Church Schools ...   1,140,655
         ,,   ,, *Dissenters'* ,,   ...   47,287
                                              ———————
                          Total ...   1,187,942
                                              ———————

These figures are unfair to the dissenters and were repudi-
ated [7] by the National Society, which represented church
opinion. It may be fairer to say that possibly " out of every
ten children of school age, four went to no school at all, three
went to Sunday schools only, two attended the very unsatisfactory dame and common day schools and one only received
an education [8] which at least escaped the strictures of the
committee " that made a survey of Manchester children's
education, and these figures must not be far removed from the
average for the whole country. If anything is clear from this
it is that the voluntary system, comparatively speaking, was

wholly inadequate without rapid extension to offer what we should consider a satisfactory provision of education in England, but until 1833 private philanthropy, and not the state, alone had a hand in education in this country. There was widespread opposition to the principle of popular elementary education, above all from the farmers and petty employers of child labour apart, of course, from the parents. Even Rousseau did not favour the education of the poor and Cobbett savagely attacked it in the House. But until the law of the land required compulsory attendance the deciding factors were the parents. In 1842 one of Her Majesty's Inspectors wrote:[9] "Strange as the truth may be, I believe that one of the greatest, if not the greatest, hindrances to education comes from those who ought to be the most forward to support it—*from the parents of the children.*" (Italics quoted.)

The National Society acting for the church, with the British and Foreign School Society, founded by Benthamites and Quakers and incorporating the Royal Lancasterian Association, acting for most of the nonconformists, largely divided the field between them. They tried to provide the nation with a satisfactory scheme of elementary education through the force of voluntary effort. The National Society, with the Archbishop of Canterbury as *ex-officio* President, has always stood for the official policy of the church in elementary education,[10] as it does even more formally to-day, although minor groups of church-people have diverted their allegiance.[11] The other great society has always received anglican support, since many inside the church have felt closer ties with their evangelical brethren amongst the nonconformists (especially the methodists) than they have with the type of thought familiar to us in Hooker and the later Caroline divines.

The success of the nonconformist educational pioneer Lancaster had caused Mrs. Trimmer, a leading advocate of church education, to insist that the church ran the risk of losing her hold upon elementary education, and the divisions of the outside world began prominently to figure in the schoolroom. It is easy to condemn Mrs. Trimmer, but a good case can be made out that the church more truly represented the nation than did any other body or even the dissenters as a whole, and the education of the nation's children should be in the principles of the national church. *The Account of*

the Proceedings at the founding of the National Society
says that " it must be admitted in this country of civil and
religious liberty that every man has a right to pursue the plan
of education that is best adapted to the religion which he himself professes."

But the same right, it is often forgotten, allows those who
subscribe in any real sense to anglican formularies, to secure
specific church teaching for church children. As time went
on the church included a progressively smaller proportion of
the people, but there was a firmer insistence on the spiritual
claims of the church. With their growing self-consciousness
the dissenting bodies brought about a wider cleavage between
church and people : the state stepped in between to make
increasing claims in the field of education. It almost seems
as though the church by her claims of privilege during the
nineteenth century partly created her own opponents, since
she fought for a political control as of right which might have
been hers by consent if her inspiration had deserved it. There
was ample recognition in many cases of the fine work of the
clergy as individuals.

The Roman catholics still suffered from very real disabilities
and only wished to live their own lives, for the transition
from the era of Milner to that of Wiseman which ushered
in Catholic expansion had not yet arrived.[12] The Wesleyans
still stood out from the British and Foreign School Society
because they desired their own distinctive teaching to be preserved and not lost in undenominationalism : [13] the same was
true of the Independents or Congregationalists, for whom
" liberty " was the breath of life. They feared that any
relationship with the state might impair the autonomy of
individual congregations. In 1820 Lord Brougham had proposed something like a national system of state education, but
under clerical control, and no progress was made. None of
the religious groups, not even the Government itself, had any
conception of the magnitude of their task. They did not
know how to face it, nor really understand its necessity. There
were, indeed, those who saw " the revolution " everywhere
and would educate the masses in order to tame them, and
there were those who would educate the masses in order to
arm them. But for the most part secularists, who made up
the latter class, showed their usual sterility, although in some
cases lack of financial resources alone prevented them from
putting high ethical ideals into practice, and for the next

thirteen years the decision as to whether elementary education was to be denominational or not was continually put off. And if the former, what was the church's position to be?

In 1833 the voluntary system was accepted by Lord John Russell as a satisfactory basis for state subsidy and building grants for elementary schools were made to the two societies, the anglican National Society and nonconformist British and Foreign School Society. The other school societies did not get a penny of this public money, nor did those who had no religion at all, the secularist reformers. These years were largely a period of stagnation for the church—Keble's assize sermon summoned the hosts to the sound of the trumpet but they assembled slowly.

Outside, the world was in a ferment of opinion. Humanitarians and evangelicals like Ashley-Cooper (Shaftesbury) worked for fundamental privileges for human beings, the radicals Cobbett and Hume, and Roebuck sought by political effort for a state of things that the ethical and utopian Owen would achieve by social action, the individualist Place who forsook his experiment in education for politics, the doctrinaire writers Ricardo and Hodgskin confronted the utilitarians and Benthamites under the two Mills, and the Chartists after their virtual defeat in 1848 showed their essentially social as well as political character by turning more and more to education: Lovett is a good example.

If the social structure of early Victorian England seemed rock-like and those who saw the mob threatening did not cease to consolidate the fabric, there were subtle forces at work in the process of disintegration. Even Carlyle, Dickens and Ruskin were subversive of the current belief in *laisser-faire*, and were all the more dangerous since they worked from within. The old order of privilege in which the church figured so prominently was breaking up, and the church itself was to stir from slumber. The stage was set for a drama not yet played out, in which the twin antitheses, alike only in having a sense of the apocalyptic, the Christian and personal kingdom of God of Maurice facing the secular and economic political state of Marx, were soon to assume their modern form.

B

I. THE CHURCH AND ELEMENTARY EDUCATION

A. THE CONSTITUTIONAL POSITION OF THE CHURCH OF ENGLAND IN 1833

BEFORE any attempt is made to study the work of the church in the nineteenth century one very important point must be made. Until the end of the War of 1914–18 the church was not free to put her house in order, since there was no real legislative and executive machinery, such as we have to-day, to make the best of her resources. Establishment conferred no privileges in the matter of education comparable with its disadvantages.

To-day there are some who complain that the multiplication of departments at headquarters—the convocations, the national assembly, the diocesan and ruri-decanal conferences, the hosts of societies, boards and committees, all taking up more and more of the time of the bishops and most business-like of the clergy, are detrimental to the church. It may be so : certainly it is in marked contrast to the state of affairs in the eighteenth and early nineteenth centuries.

Walpole's, or rather the Whig, policy of muzzling the church in order to preserve the existing social system had become an evil tradition.[1] The church had no voice and consequently little corporate sense. It was legally a vast collection of corporations sole, for the most part, and a reformer had no chance of haranguing his colleagues. Concerted action, even deliberation, or official pronouncements by the church as a body, were impossible. The paralysing effect of all this upon the individual clergy, scattered up and down the land, largely isolated units out of touch with each other for all professional purposes, can hardly be exaggerated. The Gilbertian situation then arose that the church was subjected to bitter attacks from outside on two scores which logically cancelled each other. The one was directed against the torpor of the deadened establishment and the other against the church revival under the tractarians.[2]

The church of England's strength had been the parochial system, but this was rendered in many places inadequate or

8

obsolete by the developments of the industrial revolution. Consequently there was a tendency for the church schools to be relatively much stronger in the older rural than in the newer urban areas. This happened at a time when the towns rather than the countryside were becoming dominant owing to their economic and political importance, a fact which also goes far to explain the decline in the church's influence during the century. The urban gap in the church's provision of elementary education was soon the object of special attention by the Committee of Council on Education, and the state was able to step in where the church was powerless to effect strategic planning. What good work was done resulted from individual effort for the most part, exercised at a time when successive governments had not set themselves to increase the church's power in the field of education. Nor was there for the clergy the stimulus of an appreciative or sympathetic public opinion.

Yet one important truth we may overlook is that the voluntary system, in which the church's pioneering played by far the leading part, was the basis and model on which very largely the state edifice was reared. Conversely, it may be said that only politicians could have thought of a device like " payment by results." An impartial student of the sources for the history of this period of education can hardly fail to marvel at the volume of work that the clergy did perform, and he will realize that there is another picture of the English church in 1833, different from that painted either by the compilers of the *Extraordinary Black Book* of ecclesiastical abuses or by those who wish to provide a darker background against which to portray the enlightenment of the tractarian revival.

B. THE CHURCH SCHOOL IN THE PARISH

THE nature of church elementary schools in England in 1833 was quite simple. They were, like the grammar schools, formed locally and were no concern of any one outside the parish, unless extraneous help was needed. These schools sprang up throughout the kingdom and were largely the result of clerical enterprise and not of secular or lay effort. They conformed to no plan, there were no standards as regards buildings, number and qualifications of staff, text-books (if any), fees, attendance of pupils or length of their school life, no prescribed or suggested curricula, no inspection. In fact, elementary education was a perfect example of Victorian *laisser-faire*. When almost the entire laity were indifferent the clergy alone seemed to have a care for the education of the people.

The village school was formless; it might or might not have a building of its own—a primitive schoolroom with teacher's house at best, or a home in a dame's cottage or an outbuilding of a farm, in a room at an inn, in the church vestry, even in the church itself ("but a schoolroom wanted"), in the vicarage, in a shed in a churchyard with episcopal permission, or wherever local opportunity made possible. In fact, some of these schools resembled the hedge schools of southern Ireland.

The teacher might be an ancient dame, no longer fit for aught else, an old seafaring man or broken soldier, a mere youth whom three weeks' training could be expected to transform into a successful teacher of the Madras system,[1] or a man whose sole qualification was that nothing was known against his moral character: only occasionally do we find a clergyman who had sunk so low as to keep school. Here are remarks written to an educational paper in 1851 by two schoolmasters. "That till within these few years, any poor, lame, deaf, decrepit, or broken-fortuned man who was likely to require a share of the poor rates, was considered fit for the office of schoolmaster, is a well-known fact."[2] The following explains the low standards among teachers. "It is folly to suppose young men will be induced to apply their talents to the numerous requirements laid down by the Government, unless something more is done to enhance their pay. They can easily get into the drapery, or other respectable employment, at a salary of £30, £40, or £50 per annum *with board;* while the poor school-master, with his arduous duties, is only offered £20 or £30 per year *without board.*" [3] (Italics quoted.)

The children attended spasmodically as the varying inclination of the parent, the state of the weather, the local farmers' need of child labour and many other factors permitted. Here is the verdict of an educational pioneer: " I have never known a single instance of a farmer encouraging the labourer to send his children for a longer period to school, however trifling the work for which he wanted them." [4]

We may now consider the question of the building and maintenance of the school. If the first half of the nineteenth century saw the dual rule of squire and parson but little impaired, the responsibility for seeing that the children of the poor were taught to read and write was generally felt only by the parson. We get from the National Society's survey of 1847 [5] the first complete picture, a very illuminating one, of the position in many thousands of schools scattered throughout the length and breadth of England. The one uniform note is that the expense of building, maintaining or endowing, as well as the initiative in founding, lay almost entirely with the clergy. The very first entry is that " the expense mainly falls upon the vicar," and this kind of entry largely prevails. " The education of the parish is mainly attended to by the clergyman and family, aided by several of the most respectable inhabitants," or " the school is supported by the rector entirely," or " the school is maintained by the rector and the Duke of Portland's family," relieved by such remarks as that the school is " voluntarily supported by a lady," or " there is a day school for 23 scholars maintained by the squire of the parish," whilst at Wirksworth (Derby) 50 boys in the endowed grammar school have free education.[6] A variant is that " the mistress dines at the rectory and the rector finds coals," and the entry " the free school and all parochial charities are and have been in Chancery for the last eight years and the parties responsible are dead," has a Dickensian sound. But we may continue: " With the exception of children's pence the school is entirely supported by the rector," or " There is no school. When under the care of Mr. Formby there was a Day School supported by himself," and " The School is supported by the Lord of the Manor and the children partly

clothed by him," or " A National school is much wanted.
The school is supported by the Rector." In another place,
" The incumbent has built three cottages, which he has converted into schoolrooms and dwelling for the mistress at his
own expense, with the exception of seven guineas from Mr.
and Mrs. Twopenny," whilst elsewhere " The present Sunday
schools are dependent on the Manchester Church Education
Society." Here it may be opportune to point out that the
present distinction between a week-day elementary school for
imparting mainly secular instruction and the Sunday school
for specifically religious teaching did not hold good at this
time. There is no hard and fast rule, but Sunday schools, Sunday and week-day evening schools were frequently available
for teaching children and adults who were not free to go to the
day school. Reading was taught in all schools, but in a few
writing was excluded.

This state of affairs has its positive side as showing that
where full day-time attendance was precluded by various
circumstances, a second-best was aimed at. We have mentioned the farmer's distrust of educating the poor, which was
a most potent factor, as notorious as it was widespread. There
was also middle-class prejudice against popular education.
And Lord Londonderry is quoted as saying in the House of
Lords : " Enthusiastic advocates for the education of the
labouring classes " forget " that our fields could not be
ploughed, our mines wrought, nor our ships sailed by the
use of the pen alone. The national community might be
compared to a great machine or manufactory, all its wheels
and parts must be daily proportioned to enable it to move
smoothly and the requisite proportion of education would
always be supplied without making all this stir and effort
about it. If it should preponderate, the equilibrium of
society would be destroyed." [7] This passed as a defence of
employers who needed cheap labour, and there were other
conflicting forces in the village school. The parents often
merely wanted their children temporarily out of the way at
school, while the parson desired them to learn to read their
Bible, be taught the catechism, and possibly to sing in church.
The old tradition of the schools of industry, early abandoned
by the National Society, in its crude form, still survived,
where needlework, knitting, spinning and weaving, netting,
etc. were carried on. These activities alone were regarded by
many as sufficient discipline for the children of the poor :

more literary studies were the prerogative of their betters. And it must be owned that if the matter were looked at from the realist's view-point rather than with the eye of faith the brutish life of the labourer did much to confirm this belief.

As late as 1865 there is evidence [8] of those children who wished to learn to write being required to pay an extra penny each week at Shaldon, near Teignmouth. But this was exceptional, and one of Her Majesty's Inspectors reported that " Writing is taught in all schools, and more efficiently than any other subject " in 1862.[9]

Real progress in education was being made slowly. The decline in the number of Sunday school scholars shown by the National Society's Survey of the period 1838–46 is, paradoxically, really a positive gain.[10] The decrease may be taken as an index figure of 15, compared with an increase of 180 in Sunday *and* Daily scholars, and whilst the figures do not take into account the population increase they do show that 165,000 extra children were having a full-time education instead of Sunday teaching only.

The clergy were engaged in a dull and heart-breaking struggle with apathy, prejudice and active distrust, particularly from the farming interest, as we have stressed. It is only by keeping clear this background to their activities that the volume of clerical achievement can be understood. " This school costs the clergyman near £30 and he is fearful it must be closed unless he can obtain extraneous aid " is only typical of many entries in the 1846–7 survey. There were many Mr. Formbys in this period. We may go further and say that clergy frequently considered the setting up of a school as an integral part of church extension. We quote from a letter written to the National Society in 1847 : " This chapelry is one of the most remarkable examples of church extension. Twelve years ago, we had one church, one clergyman, two Sunday services, and no National School. We have now five churches, seven clergymen, fourteen full Sunday services, five National schools in daily operation, one infant school, and a handsome subscription in progress for another National School and a master's house. And I have the happiness to report that the most friendly co-operation and good understanding prevail among us. We are but a poor people, and could not have accomplished a tithe of our good works but for the generous assistance of distant friends. We are deeply indebted to the church societies, and not least to the National Society, for their efficient aid in increasing our educational apparatus." [11]

There is evidence testifying to lay benevolence,—" This school is supported by a private individual," or even to noble beneficence,—" Schoolroom built by Lord Balcariss at an expense of £1,500." Bishop E. S. Talbot tells us [12] of his father's fulfilment of a desire to build (in Kent, about 1850) church, parsonage house and school as an entity.

Finally we may quote a Government report of 1845 : [13] " It is, however, in a few instances only that I find a decided interest in the welfare of the school manifested by the laity, or sacrifices for its support, on a scale commensurate with its importance to the public welfare, made by anybody except a clergyman.   The following is a list of the subscriptions to a village school in my district in the year 1844.   I copy it as an example of the unjust proportion in which the clergy are called upon to contribute to the support of elementary education.   It would not be difficult to cite a long list of similar examples :—

	£	s.	d.
The lord of the manor and principal landowner	3	3	0
The rector	17	10	4
The rector's lady	1	1	0
A friend of the rector	5	5	0
A farmer and landowner		5	0
,, ...		5	0
,, ...		5	0
,, ...		5	0
,, ...		10	0
,, ...		5	0
,, ...		5	0
	£28	19	4 "

It is not unreasonable to read into this financial statement, cited as typical of the condition of affairs in many parishes, the incumbent's liability to make up the deficit on the year's working. [14]   The real tragedy of the position is that so frequently the clergy were ahead of the great mass of the laity in their recognition of the nation's need for elementary schools covering the entire country, but were unable to carry the people with them.

This is the local aspect of the elementary schools set up

by individuals all over the country. Any real estimate of
the self-sacrifice necessary to provide these schools, of the
blind faith that inspired this work and of the difficulties which
had to be overcome cannot from the nature of the case be
made. Of all men, Her Majesty's Inspectors, who went round
their districts minutely inspecting schools and scholars, should
be the fittest witnesses to the educational effort of the clergy.
Here is a verdict passed in 1842 : [15] " I feel that I cannot
conclude this Report without returning to say a few words
on the clergy in their parish schools . . . I have looked carefully over my lists, and I can find only nine instances out of
nearly 200, where I have not reason to think that the clergyman has a deep interest in his school, not shown only by
words, but by watchful care and frequent attendance.   I
could mention instances, where, after morning religious instruction in the day school, the clergyman teaches the school
at night; others where, when the master has been ill, or
absent for some time, the clergyman has cheerfully supplied
his place, lest the school should suffer loss; others again
where, besides labour almost beyond his strength, pecuniary
help beyond his means has been cheerfully given, poor children paid for, masters' stipends made up to a certain income,
repairs done, as it were, by stealth, debts willingly taken upon
himself, and contributions offered, liberal to excess, that
others might be moved to contribute liberally.   These, I am
thankful, I have witnessed frequently in my late tour of
inspection.   I am convinced that no one could see what I
have seen, of the truly charitable work of the clergy for the
support and success of these schools, without feeling increased
respect for them.   There are, I know, some who are yet
asleep, but I trust that they will be soon awakened from their
sleep, and will rise and be doing."

If Newman's remark that those who attack the church owe
it to the church that they are able to articulate at all is rather
harsh, we may say without fear of contradiction that it is in
the main due to the church that those developments in
elementary education which to-day shut us off from a proper
understanding of the state of affairs in the period immediately
after 1833 have arisen. This was Dean Hook's view : [16] " We
have lighted a lanthorn which only makes us more sensible of
the surrounding darkness." The church, then, largely raised
by her own efforts the criteria by which many later critics
have condemned her work for its very inadequacy.

We may now turn to consider the church's parish elementary schools from the national standpoint. More and more these isolated units came into relationship with the National Society. Some schools, it is true, had no connexion with the Society in any way, others were in sympathy with its objects but did not formally enter into union, yet the great majority seem so to have entered, either directly or indirectly, with the local associations. This was especially true after 1833, when the Society became the medium for administering the Government grant for church schools. We may glance at the history of the National Society in its early years.

C. THE EARLY YEARS OF THE NATIONAL SOCIETY TO 1839

THIS Society had been founded, as we have seen, in 1811 by members of the Society for Promoting Christian Knowledge, such as Joshua Watson. The S.P.C.K. had in the eighteenth century done much good work in setting up schools, and these founders brought with them something of the S.P.C.K. tradition. Until 1829 the latter ran its own schools, when it left the field clear by a division of function to the National Society.[1] The duty of the Society was to co-ordinate the work of the church elementary schools throughout England (and Wales) by every possible means. It made cash grants for building schools, maintained model and demonstration schools for the training of teachers, and incidentally held annual " open days " for the supporters of the Society, and helped the cause of church elementary education generally as it saw new opportunities open to it. Above all, it never failed to remind church people of their responsibilities for the education of the poor in church principles. The society accepted schools, on certain conditions,[2] into union with itself, thus linking them up into a loose national federation without destroying either their voluntary or local character.

We may just briefly remark that between 1811 and 1834 the society gave to church schools in building grants a sum of £105,000. Three times this sum was added locally by those responsible for erecting new schools, the total cost being well over four hundred thousand pounds. The entire cost of all these buildings cannot be ascertained for they were purely the result of local effort and no records exist : similarly there are no figures for the cost of maintaining these schools. For what it is worth we subjoin the following table, but it must be stressed that these figures apply only to schools in actual union with the National Society.

Year.	In Sunday and Daily Schools.		In Sunday Schools.		Schools in Union.	Total Scholars.
	Boys.	Girls.	Boys.	Girls.		
1835.	178,740.	145,305.	93,929.	98,207.	5,559.	516,181.

Further to stress the vague classification of the time we notice that in the abstract of returns made to Parliament in 1833 a total of 154 schools not on the National Society's list returned

17

themselves as " National " schools.[3]   In addition to the schools
in union the Society had in 1835 sixty local associations of
unpaid helpers to promote the cause of elementary education,[4]
employing the local and voluntary principle of the later School
Boards.   During the years 1811–34 these little societies gave
£20,000 [5]—a sum equalling the entire Government grant of
the year 1834—for building schools, although finance was
only one of their main concerns.[6]   These sums are " independent of the occasional assistance given to schools for the
training of masters, and on other accounts, and also of a very
large number of National schools which have been established
and provided with schoolrooms by private persons, and of
many endowed schools which have been enlarged and thrown
open to the public by trustees, who although they are acting
generally upon the Society's principles and plans have not
hitherto formally entered into union."   There were in 1835
two central schools under the National Society at Westminster
and forty-three in the country for training teachers : 2,000
persons have been reported to the society as having been
trained at these centres.   The following table may be cited : [7]

Teachers in Training at the Westminster Central Schools.

	Masters.	Mistresses.
Teachers on Probation at own request	91	80
Teachers received into training from local boards	41	32
Teachers provided with permanent posts	70	70
Teachers sent to temporary charge of schools	32	32

We may now examine the work of the National Society more
closely, and from the inside, as it were.   The early Minute
Books rather than the condensed annual reports should be
carefully studied if we are to understand not only the nature
and scope of the National Society's work, but what is more
important to a student of Christian institutions, the spirit that
informed it.

The minutes of " The National Society for Promoting the
Education of the Poor in the Principles of the Established
Church " are carefully written out in long hand and signed by
the chairman of the committee for the meeting, His Grace of
Canterbury or York or a diocesan bishop, very occasionally
a layman like Mr. Trimmer, and even after this lapse of time
they have a personal flavour.   In the year 1833 the Society's

committee has before it at every meeting requests from local parish schools to be taken into union, but points out that it is contrary to the practice of the Society to form a connexion with daily schools only as distinct from Sunday and daily schools, since the society's aim was primarily to further church life rather than to impart mere secular instruction. Grants were made to schools on long lists, and it is typical of the combination of piety and a genuine concern also for the physical welfare of the little children the committee can never expect to see that they require as a condition of a subsidy to a parish school that the Sunday ministrations shall be given voluntarily and the height of the schoolroom increased. A sum of £100 is granted to an applicant as he has himself endowed the school, whilst a pension of £52 is granted to a mistress of twenty years' service. The history of teachers' pensions would show this as a princely gesture. The Disposable Balance is £1,641 plus £2,739 from the King's Letter, making a total of £4,480. The King's Letter (later the Queen's) was an appeal, to be read in every parish church at the royal command, for charitable causes, of which the National Society was one.[8] The Queen's Letter ceased in 1855. When the Queen's ministers would no longer advise its continuance, although it was solely addressed to church people in their churches for church objects, the archbishops and bishops co-operated in an appeal to the church at large for the National Society.[9]

It is possible to regard the action of the Government as a declaration that it could not help the church, or at any rate a society, to perpetuate its work in a sphere more properly belonging to the state. Or conceivably there was fear of the charge of denominationalism. The schools alone suffered from this petty act.

Next month 7,000 returns have been received, bringing in £19,856. In assessing the amount to be granted to a parish the committee is guided partly by the volume of local effort: about £40 was an average sum. Dr. Bell's portrait is sent to Lambeth, property is newly acquired at Westminster, books are given as school prizes, and a reference made to the Parliamentary building grant for schools, and thanks given to clergy who have set up schools without the aid of the National Society. The following year (1834) a sum of £100 per annum is promised by the King and £300 " arrears " are enclosed along with the donation for the current year. Cases of deficiency in local funds for building schools are sent to the Treasury, and in turn My Lords forward a list of schools to be paid £7,200 through the Society. A request is made to the Treasury for free covers for a circular letter to all incumbents with over 1,500 souls in their care explaining the work of the National Society. Certificates are drafted for those desirous of starting Infant Schools, the Secretary replies to two Roman Catholic schools who make a pathetic application that he cannot help them, and the Treasury is notified of new schools to be built at a cost of £75,742 and showing a deficiency of £33,673, and it is noted that applications from schools already built but not yet paid for cannot be considered. The Treasury's £20,000 is soon exhausted and Government can only consider cases of towns with a population of 5,000 or over. A significant indication of contemporary standards is the school at Roade :

a room 35′ × 21′ will house 120 children
a room 30′ × 16′ will house 80 children.

An enterprising incumbent at Reading has made " a moveable school-room " constructed " on the principle of the houses sent out to Van Dieman's Land and the Colonies "—precursor of the modern Army hut. At an early meeting in 1835 grants are made conditionally upon local men of substance offering guarantees. The Society, indeed, is continually reminding itself and others of how little it can do with its present resources, and draws up a long list of towns and shows the proportion of church scholars to population. These are some figures taken at random from the minutes :

Bexley has	3,500	people and	320	church scholars	
Bootle has	22,575	„	„	150	„	„
Deptford has	20,000	„	„	100	„	„
Ilchester has	1,020	„	„	240	„	„
Marylebone has	122,208	„	„	330	„	„

Newcastle-on-Tyne Sunday School Society is taken into union, and the Committee makes a sympathetic reply to a Treasury query about the establishment of model schools : the latter can now give an annual maximum of 10/- per scholar in grants. The society is ever watchful and the bishop of Exeter is asked to revive instruction at the *daily* school at Tiverton, whilst the society is concerned that in the Scilly Isles the S.P.C.K. is making a grant for daily work *only*—Sunday and week-day schools are regarded as being complementary to each other. Four schools are able to refuse £203 from the Treasury, since they can manage to pay their way without it. The Society sends further information by request to the Treasury about model schools and asks whether it may expect a grant for its new departure—the training of teachers. In March, 1836, the Society is seriously concerned over the fact that 3,007 places figuring separately in population returns are without schools: at every turn it is hampered by lack of funds. A gratuity of £25 and a note of appreciation are sent to a mistress compelled to retire and another novel feature is the committee's consideration of the supply of Infant Teachers. This question of teachers worries the committee: a matron and houses are secured for " the females in attendance " at the society's model schools to be trained as teachers. An unusual feature is the withdrawal of a school—at Liss—despite the incumbent's efforts, but good reports come from Brighton of the chimney-sweeps' class there. The Ripon clergy in 1837 form their own Diocesan Education Society in union with the National Society and having their own model schools, a mistress's bill of £10 8s. for medical care in her illness is met by the society, and a prize given to a schoolmaster.

The committee of the National Society is ever alert to seize new opportunities of meeting the educational needs of the people. The bishops of London and Winchester discuss a plan for giving a religious and " commercial " or general education to the middle classes: could this be done on a large scale and could not " diocesan seminaries " for young teachers be set up everywhere? It is now, however, perfectly clear that such projects were long in advance of their time, for neither church nor nation was ready for such suggestions. The committee suggests that schoolmasters should be trained and licensed by the bishop, but they should also be adequately paid and comfortably housed, promoted according to merit and pensioned after proper service. Moral songs for the children would also be a welcome innovation, and in five more places *daily* as well as Sunday school instruction is urged. The committee is worried by the lack of text-books and is to prepare a suitable list of books for the guidance of teachers, is reassured that the Society does not risk forfeiting its charter by helping middle-class schools, and continues to negotiate with the Treasury about model schools. In eight dioceses there are school boards,[10] three are in process of being formed, whilst seven diocesan training colleges are to be established:

at Lichfield is a diocesan commercial school. In the dioceses of Norwich and Ely one inspector visits 25 schools and in this year, 1839, the S.P.C.K. gives the society £5,000 for its work, and the London Diocesan Board of Education is formed, chiefly through Bishop Blomfield.[11] It is felt that the Society cannot afford to help the middle school at Leeds, as this should depend on local effort by a class better fitted to shift for itself. Then the most important question of inspection of schools is raised by the Society, and the Treasury is asked what help it can give. Three sub-committees—of schools, of finance, and of correspondence—are set up. Next the question of state intrusion extorts a firm letter from the National Society to the Committee of Council relative to the terms of the Government grant. The Committee of Council is given details of the proposed collegiate institution for 50–60 school-masters and hope is entertained of a similar one for females. Finally, in November, 1839, the committee of the National Society agrees to publish the correspondence between its own correspondence sub-committee and the Committee of Council on the very vexed question of the inspection of schools : the National Society is to nominate a suitable inspector to His Grace of Canterbury.

With this sample of the minutes of the Society we may leave the narrow compass of its own story for a wider topic. Henceforward the National Society is concerned with consolidating its position rather than with expanding the scope of its activities and the prophetic note tends to disappear. And a careful watch is kept on the giant new intruder : Cæsar must be jealously guarded lest he step aside from his own proper function now that in the Committee of Council on Education he has his own instrument of action.

But this leads to the conflict of opinion in the church itself on the whole question of elementary education, a struggle which, however unedifying it may seem in some respects, was both productive of many new ideas and is the best evidence of the vitality of churchmen's interest and convictions.

D. THE CONFLICT OF CHURCH OPINION ON THE QUESTION OF ELEMENTARY EDUCATION

A CONVICTION is held by many people, and is sufficiently general to be worthy of formal statement and refutation, that there were two widely divergent streams of thought on the subject of elementary education in the last century. There was the state policy that ultimately bore fruit, if that is the right word, in the School Boards and a determination to " stand no nonsense " from the church. Parallel and opposed to this was the determination of the established church to abide in the ways of her ancient privilege and keep the dissenters—who had already produced an educational administrator of genius in Kay-Shuttleworth [1]—strictly in their place. This view is simple and adds the merit of being comforting, but it is not historical. In the first place, of course, Sir James Kay-Shuttleworth was an adult convert, like F. D. Maurice, to the English church from unitarianism and his life and works were the fruit of his Christian faith. In addition, it would be difficult to formulate a definite and coherent philosophy of state education from Lord John Russell to Mr. Birrell. The state, in fact, lumbered along behind the machinery of the voluntary system until Mr. Lowe put the brake on everybody. Mr. Gladstone assured the religious bodies that the Government was merely supplementing their efforts and Mr. Forster then stole a march on them all in 1870.

And what of the church? He would be a bold man who would talk of a " church policy." There was the National Society, supported by the mass of church people, whose position has been stated : " . . . in the abeyance of synods, Church societies become, very unfortunately, as I think, but, doubtless, very unavoidably, Committees upon various Church matters." [2] But even here opinion had been divided, and as early as 1833 the good and honest Joshua Watson, one of its founders, resigned from the National Society rather than compromise his conscience and the principle of church education by accepting a Government grant. He regarded the state's incursion into education as an invasion of the province of the purely spiritual. He was the heir of a great Christian

23

tradition that mistrusted (and nowhere more than men did in presbyterian Scotland) all state activities in religious matters. Further, the Society was attacked in many ways for contradictory reasons, and although there is no point in reviving long-dead controversies, this conflict of ideas and ideals has its value in showing from what sources later policy sprang. Thomas Arnold of Rugby declined to join with the National Society,[3] which did not fit in with his Latitudinarianism, and we are credibly informed[4] that Dr. Edward Stanley, bishop of Norwich and father of the dean, offered a large accession of funds to the National Society provided the teaching of the Church Catechism were left optional. In 1851 John Keble presented a memorial to the Society, however, on the shortcomings of many clergy in not insisting on the teaching of the catechism.[5] Worse than this was a schism : " Dissatisfied with his position on the Committee, where he was in a decided minority . . . Mr. Colquhoun tendered his resignation in July, 1852 ; and early in the following year he reappeared before the public as the founder of a rival society, which, as regardless of honesty as it had been of peace, abrogated to itself the name of ' The Church of England Education Society.'[6] The injury thus done to the cause of Church Education was aggravated in the same year by a violent outcry, raised by the promoters of the new society, against the customary issue of the Royal Letter in favour of the old established Church Education Society."[7] This move led to the cessation of the Queen's Letter.

The Revd. Richard Burgess (1796–1881) represented a large body of clergy who took a " national " rather than " church " view of the elementary education question.[8] He states that " The necessity of a free, cheap and general system of education for the poorer classes of this country, arises from their present physical and moral condition, which every enlightened and benevolent mind must deplore." His opinion is that " the Voluntary System, in providing for the spiritual instruction of the country, is failing every day : to attempt the moral and religious education of the poorer classes in the same way, would be to attempt an utter impossibility." His solution of the problem is simple : the responsibility for national education rests with the State. But the Government must also give pledges to the clergy of its intention of setting up a " Christian " system of education. In assessing the work of the voluntary system Burgess compared educational statistics in England and Prussia and pointed the moral. He called for a system of national elementary education which was simultaneously to be in the hands of the state and yet to be truly Christian.

A writer and thinker whose greatness and prophetic genius mark him as one of the seminal minds of the century was Frederick Denison Maurice (1805–72). [9] His views on education, in some fields of which he was himself a pioneer, cannot lightly be dismissed. They are thoroughly uncompromising, but F. D. Maurice always tried to escape from the crowded arena of the temporal in order to see things under the guise of eternity. For example, whereas Archdeacon Denison was wont to stress the church's claims, Maurice ever urged her responsibilities before God. In 1839 Maurice delivered a course of lectures on the question: *Has the Church or the State the Power to Educate the Nation?* Here on page 129 of this work is a typical statement: " No cowardice, putting on the face of modesty, shall prevent us from declaring that we have a commission, and authority, and ability, to educate the whole mind of the country: a power of forming the nation, which those who would take upon themselves our duties do not and cannot possess. No shame for past misuse of the trust which has been committed to us, shall tempt us to the further sin of denying that we retain it. But at the same time we are bound, by the most solemn obligations, to make our pretensions good, to prove that they are not put forth rashly or proudly for the sake of self-display, or that we may retain selfish honours, but in the firm belief that the tenure by which we hold our gifts is not one that makes them dependent on our individual merits any more than upon State patronage, but one that ensures our continual renewal of the only strength in which we are able to exercise them for the good of this age or for posterity." But Maurice has no sectarian prejudices: [10] " You have always a vague notion that we want you to do something for us—in some way or other to help us against the sects. We ask no such thing. . . . We are born in an age in which men are trying to find a bond of union for themselves, and cannot find it—in which they are abusing one another for not being conciliatory, and are ready to tear one another in pieces for the sake of establishing charity. We are born in an age of parties—it is God's will that it should be so: we cannot make it otherwise by not believing it. We (Churchmen) have an education which

assumes men to be members of one family—of one nation.
(A family we declare to be universal, limited by no conditions of time or country; to belong to it is our great human
privilege. This principle underlies all our education, and is
the very meaning of it! Only on such a foundation can a
united nation be built. We have learned, therefore, to reverence our own function more, but it is the function of pro-
claiming truth to men : and we have come to think less and
less of your State machinery, because it carries with it no such
power.) If any persons like to be educated on that ground,
we will educate them ; if they do not like it, they must educate
themselves upon what other principle they may, for we know
of no other. The State rushes in and says, ' But we can.
We will make you members of one family, whether you like
it or not. You shall love by Act of Parliament, and embrace
it by an Order in Council. You have paid for our protection ;
of course, therefore, we are bound in honour to make you
wise and charitable.' This is their scheme ; I believe that
it will work in this way. It will teach those who are indifferent
to be more indifferent, . . . more intolerant, . . . (and result in)
the nation growing . . . more divided and broken."

Maurice wrote on the question of responsibility for the
present state of popular education : " The ablest speakers in
both houses of Parliament in the late debates rested their case
on this ground : ' The English poor are in a state of wretched
ignorance, you have not cured it—we must.' These words,
I believe, contain a summary of all that was said in support
of government interference. . . . If the members of the
legislature call upon us to confess the evils which we witness
around us as national sins for which we are all responsible
who have had any influence to exert them, for which we,
above all others, are responsible—I rejoice that they have
estimated our condition so truly. I shall not complain that
such acknowledgments have come first from our statesmen.
I shall not say that they are at all departing from their office
in uttering them. Every man who feels himself a member of
the nation has a right to utter them, and it would be a
delightful change from the cold, heartless spirit which has
characterized us so long, if we began, one and all of us, to
feel bitter shame for our past misdoings, not trying to shift
the disgrace of them upon our fathers; not wishing to
represent them as the effect of inevitable circumstances : but
frankly, and from our inmost hearts, owning that we, our

priests, our kings, our nobles, every man among us, have failed of our duty, and are suffering, and must suffer, the appointed punishment." [11]

The church at large, the episcopate and clergy and most of the thinking laity, probably regarded the matter of elementary education from the standpoint of their responsibility as pastors or leaders. They had to superintend the active provision of church teaching primarily as a means of imparting religious dogma—the beliefs that shall be the basis of our actions.

Other churchmen took a less ecclesiastical view, seeing their duty in a more secular setting: such a man was W. F. Hook (1798–1875), at this time vicar of Leeds. Hook was one of the most vigorous of parish priests, and he now wrote a pamphlet, in the form of an open letter, to Connop Thirlwall, Bishop of St. Davids,[12] a kindred spirit, condemning the existing popular education as highly unsatisfactory because it was utterly inadequate. Hook's letter has been described as coming like a bombshell, and later students of the history of elementary education have paid much attention to it. In effect, what Hook did was to criticize most severely the whole voluntary system, blessed by the hierarchy and accepted by the state. *Fidelia vulnera amantis.*

" I admit with gratitude the good which has been accomplished through the instrumentality of the National Society. I concede with pleasure the credit which is due to dissenting societies, especially to the Methodists. I demand the praise of all unprejudiced men for the indefatigable zeal in the cause of education, speaking generally of the clergy." [13] But in comparison with the educational needs of the country Hook claimed that next to nothing had been done. This is hardly a fair statement of the position. The evidences of achievement furnished by the voluntary societies are minimized as *ex parte* statements which advertise the good work undoubtedly done, but must be received with caution as omitting defects. Amongst these Hook reckons " duplicate entries " of pupils in returns of statistics, and suggests that "insecured" school buildings, where there is no legal guarantee of permanent tenure for educational purposes, give an unduly optimistic view of the position. In both of these matters we now know that the National Society was anxious to state the whole truth.[14] Unfortunately Hook's charges are more familiar to students of this subject than the evidence refuting them.

" Proceeding to consideration of the *quality* of our education, I must begin by remarking that we possess some admirable schools. I have schools in my own parish which might challenge comparison with any schools anywhere established. If I were employed as an advocate of the present system of education, I might appeal to our bitterest opponent, and if he has common feelings of honesty, he would freely admit that we have done much more than, with our scanty resources, he could have supposed to be possible. But where are these schools to be found? In localities inhabited by the wealthy : in districts where the clergy are not only active, but numerous and influential, and where a laity possessing leisure are willing to discharge gratuitously the office of teacher or at least of inspectors. But go to our poorer districts, not to our towns but to our manufacturing villages and there you perceive how great our educational destitution really is. I am myself surrounded by a district containing 250,000 souls, exclusive of the large towns, in which there are thousands uneducated, or receiving an education worse than none; for where a number of children are gathered together, if some good is not going on, much of evil must ensue from the mere aggregation of numbers. Not one in a hundred attends any place of worship, but the usual practice is for the men to lie in bed on the Sunday morning, while the women cook the dinner, and for an adjournment in the evening to take place to a public house." [15]

Hook is, of course, perfectly right : these great new centres of industrial population largely grew up outside the pale of the church, which as we have mentioned had no machinery for keeping its organization abreast of developments. What were the clergy doing? " The very first object which a respectable clergyman has in view when he receives an appointment is to form a school. But, suppose him to be placed in one of those poor districts which abound in the land, in which there is no man of wealth resident, what is he to do? Let us suppose him by great exertion to have obtained a pittance sufficient to pay for the hire of a room, having calculated on collecting three or four pounds every year by a charity sermon (little as this seems to be, the collection often is less): let us suppose him to have induced some pious young man, for the love of God, to give up a trade, and to undertake the school with a trifling salary, and with the hope of obtaining a livelihood by the pence of the children. The poor young man having been sent to that apology for a training school at Westminster, has confided to him as a great privilege, the sole charge of 100 or 150 little dirty, ragged, ignorant urchins, assembled in the miserable building now dignified by the name of a National School Room, and he is expected, as by a miracle, to convert them, in as short a space of time as possible, into clean, well-bred, intelligent children, capable of passing a creditable examination, if by chance an inspector or organizing master pass that way. He begins his work upon these hundred or 150 children, and upon whom does he depend for assistance and support? The clergyman of the parish or district looks in occasionally, and gives him a word of encouragement, but the multiplicity of his various and important duties prevents his doing more; or he thinks, perhaps, that his friend the schoolmaster is the only person in his district upon whose co-operation in works of piety he can depend, and consequently so far from aiding the schoolmaster he looks to the schoolmaster for assistance. And in the school what can the good young man effect? He cannot educate (it is physically impossible) all the children himself, and therefore he is obliged to have recourse to the monitorial system: the result of which is, while a portion of the children are vain, conceited and puffed-up, a larger proportion are left in their ignorance. I have known instances of children who have been for two years at a National School, and have left it unable to read. The master seeing this, depressed in spirit, gets through the drudgery of the school hours as best he may; but has his work ceased? No; he must teach his monitors; to them he must impart some knowledge out of school hours, and his mind is still kept on the stretch. He may also be under the necessity of keeping an evening school. Nor is he even then at rest. Having lamented the inconvenience of the room they have hired for a school, he and the clergyman are found closeted together, devising the best means, from a letter to the Queen Dowager down to the holding of a bazaar, for erecting a building better suited to their purpose. They determine to beg. The principal burden of this begging devolves upon the clergyman. The master, too, is employed in this work; and though he finds himself regarded as one who has no fixed station in society, he very often by his patience and perseverance succeeds wonderfully. They labour incessantly until at last, by the aid of the National Society, a grant from the Committee of Council and a liberal donation from Queen Adelaide, the requisite amount is nearly gained. The clergyman then proceeds to build, and guarantees the money that is wanted to complete the work, which, generally speaking, he has to pay from his private resources. There is no complaint to be made; both clergyman and master feel that they have been labouring in their vocation, and in labouring for the glory of God, and the welfare of their fellow creatures. . . . Nor is the anxiety of the master to cease with the completion of the building: upon him, equally with the clergyman, devolves the duty of collecting the subscriptions needful to defray the expenses; and he has always the prospect before him of being reduced to greater want, at the very time that his family is increasing, by the defalcation of the pence of the children, upon which, either wholly or in part, his subsistence is made to depend. From increase of the population, the clergyman, meanwhile, as soon as one school is built, has to commence another, and when all is done, he has the satisfaction of feeling that it is as only a drop in the ocean! " [16]

Hook was not, of course, allowed to state this case and remain challenge free. Attacks came from churchmen on all sides who respected and admired Hook, [17] yet could not agree with his revolutionary criticisms. But before dealing with these we must first consider Hook's specific reference to the inadequacy of the National Society's training of teachers. On page 62 of this very letter there is a decided eulogy of the society's colleges, St. Mark's, Battersea and Whitelands, Chelsea. This is only a small part of what was being done: there are thirteen training institutions all " efficiently conducted," of which three are to be enlarged. [18] An example of work of a different kind was the holding of " refresher courses " for teachers, which will be mentioned in greater detail elsewhere. [19]

The statistics of teachers directly trained by the National Society may be of interest. They certainly bear out as far as they are relevant the truth of Hook's contention, for an annual intake of 208 trained teachers from the five main institutions was far from satisfactory. [20] Contemporary criticism, however, is mainly adverse. A statistical reply was attempted in *Some remarks on a letter addressed by the Rev. Dr. Hook . . . By one of the " Clergy of the Manufacturing District " and parish of Manchester*, containing

135 pages and published in 1846. But Hook in putting his
finger on " manufacturing villages and districts " was thinking
not of towns like Leeds or villages proper, but new developments such as those at Yeadon and Guiseley.[21]   The Rev.
Wm. Harness [22] even thought Hook was joking and insisted
that party differences rendered any unified scheme impossible,
apart from the cost of three million pounds.[23]   He speaks
feelingly of Sunday schools :   " To this eminently popular
method of profaning the Sabbath, I have always entertained
the most decided aversion."   Preb. J. B. M. Clarke [24] paid
tribute to the vicar of Leeds' character and good works, while
strongly defending the voluntary system :   his attitude seems
to have been typical of that of most clergy.   The Rev. R.
Burgess, D.D., somewhat surprisingly, in his *Letter to the Rev.
F. W. Hook, D.D.*, thinks Hook's plan is in essence that
of the Central Education Society of 1837.   This was enough
to damn it in the eyes of most people as offering a purely
secular solution to the problem of elementary education.   In
short, it may be said that Dr. Hook's pamphlet both pointed
out the inadequacy of the voluntary system and stressed the
heroic efforts of the clergy to achieve the impossible.   There
were other critics.   A pamphlet by the Rev. Edward Girdlestone, " The Labourers' Friend," [25] (1805–1884) has a significant title :   *The Committee of Council an imaginary enemy,
a real friend*.   Published in 1850, it was a defence of the
State's activity.   Another criticism of the National Schools
will be found in the suggestions for reform, possibly published
in the same year, by an Inspector of the Oxford Diocesan
Board of Education.[26]   All parties in the educational disputes
stuck doggedly by their principles and if the unyielding spirit
of many churchmen hindered the progress of national education, precisely the same may be said of the dissenters, who
caused the rejection of Sir James Graham's Bill of 1843.

Speaking of obstructionists, we are at once reminded of
George Anthony Denison (1805–1896), Archdeacon of Taunton.   Denison was thoroughly human and tolerant, but his
convictions about the catholic nature and divine purpose of
the church led him on with relentless logic to plan and lead
attacks on every one suspected of heresy, from the Archbishop downwards.   He produced a vast amount of
polemical literature, but his views are soon made clear.
Denison's open letter to the member for the University of
Oxford,[27] the Rt. Hon. W. E. Gladstone, was written in

1847 : " . . . promoters of schools," he says, " are hesitating between their necessities and their fear of committing themselves to a vicious principle and embarrassing all their future efforts to maintain the integrity of Church teaching." As time went on, however, and the state came to play a more direct part in the provision of elementary education, Denison wrote to Canon Wordsworth another letter which may be noticed on *The Position and Prospects of the National Society*. Both the National Society and the Committee of Council are assailed, for Denison allowed of no compromise.[28] It should now be perfectly clear that the National Society was by no means synonymous with the Church of England, although supported officially by the episcopal bench, or most of it, and enjoying for long a peculiar relationship to the State. Apart from G. A. Denison, who claimed that the church " cannot consent to part with any of those rights which still remain to mark her peculiar position in the country," [29] little mention has been made of the tractarians. Individual clergy did great work but " it does not seem easy to fix on any specific educational ideal which we can associate with the followers of Newman and Pusey." [30] This seems true enough, save for the work and ideals of Woodard and Pusey's encouragement of the teaching work of the Wantage and Clewer sisterhoods.

Extremes beget their opposites, and with the growing desire for popular control of national institutions we meet much impatience with clerical management of elementary education : the mood of that Berkshire farmer who desired fewer black parsons and more black pigs. The clergy even took sides on this point and we may notice a great educationist who wrote against the work of men like Archdeacons Denison, Sinclair, and H. E. Manning, the future Cardinal : Richard Dawes (1793–1867).[31]

" The National Society, and perhaps a majority of the clergy, wish to introduce a system of education which would establish in every parish a charity school for the education of the poor—charity, which at all events as regards money matters, whatever it might be in other things—to make the face of the country a ' net-work ' of schools on eleemosynary principles, keeping the labouring classes, in their education and habits formed in early life, entirely apart from the classes immediately above them. Now, this is making a distinction of a most invidious kind, the labouring classes feel no elevation of mind in being educated in this way : on the contrary, it has a most depressing tendency about it, and they feel that it is not a thing in which they take any interest themselves, but think it the duty of the clergy to write begging letters year after year, and to preach education sermons in order to provide it ; and after all, the result, hitherto, has been satisfactory neither to the clergy nor the classes for whom it is intended . . . this form of school is so stereotyped on the minds of many, both clergy and laity, that it is become hard to introduce an improved education into our parish schools and create a feeling in favour of it ; as it would be, to introduce a new system of weights and measures, or a new coinage . . . the *vis inertiae* of the stolid forms of ignorance in bucolic life—and what may the difficulty not be ! " This is a fine human work, the product of a forward-looking mind. Dawes attacks the static church schools, comparing them unfavourably with the progressive Government schools. Too many clergy are satisfied to use the schools chiefly as a place for teaching children to read the Bible, learn the catechism and mind their manual work—as a means to perpetuating the rural *status quo*.[32]

Again Dawes attacks the National Society, saying that it " has in some measure been a national deception, retarding the cause of education rather than advancing it, by taking the place of a better system." [33] A quotation from *The Times* is given and it will illustrate an intelligent lay view of the issues between parties on the subject of elementary education : " All parties are afraid of it. Some fear the subject and some hate it : some wish nothing to be done, and some nothing to be said. The difficulty of determining between the secular and spiritual interests of humanity is fatal to the question ; and unless some sort of compromise can be speedily attained to, society bids fair to resolve itself into those who would educate every plough-boy for the pulpit, and those who would teach him nothing whatever but what will perish in the grave." [34]

These quotations hardly suggest that the lines of action were clear : certainly there is nothing true in the suggestion that the church failed in a perfectly obvious duty to further elementary education. We have no hesitation in bringing forward Dawes' condemnation of the varied opposition to the spread of popular enlightenment, especially middle-class prejudice. The church needs state help, and the state cannot manage without the church. Then the poor are ignorant of the value of education and fear it, for it was too new for experience to have proved its worth. He thinks that the country is not yet ready for local education rates, but prophesies that these will be introduced, and again he accurately forecasts the shape of things to come. Government servants such as messengers will, he thinks, have to pass a literacy test, and this stipulation, by giving it a cash value, will raise the prestige of education.[35]

On the face of it Dawes' indictment of " the eleemosynary principle " looks very convincing. When we come, however, to examine the vast mass not of mere poverty but of chronic destitution that characterized Victorian England we find that " charity " [36] in some form or other was essential, whether in the voluntary form then so common or in the shape of state subsidy, and the time was not ripe for this. Other than educational issues arise here which cannot be pursued, but it is clear that in the minds of a great many people the church's provision of popular education did expose those who received it to a consciousness of being patronized. The rapid development of half-conscious democratic aspirations led to a keen resentment against anything in the nature of a static conception of class and society. The alliance of parson and squire was often misunderstood, and being by nature conservative in outlook these latter often failed completely to understand the mind of the people. A vast amount of anti-clerical feeling is still traceable amongst an older generation to this social cause, rather than to religious differences.

E. CONTINUED PROGRESS OF THE NATIONAL SOCIETY AND THE QUESTION OF EDUCATIONAL DESTITUTION

THE provision of elementary education made steady progress in the years 1839–1847, and this is perfectly easy to gauge quantitatively from the survey in the next chapter.[1] The figures show that in ten years the proportion of the population who were daily scholars rose from 1 in 29 to 1 in 18.

The National Society claimed that if every child received *four* years of schooling the figures representing the number of children who should be found in the schools would be these.

Year.	*School Population.*	*Increase in 10 years.*
1847	2,020,083	
1837	1,832,506	187,577

The actual recorded increase in the scholars in schools in *direct* union with the National Society alone was 180,000. If the years of schooling should be raised to *eight* the figures would be increased—the 1837 school population to 2,926,512, the 1847 school population to 3,226,072, and the increase of scholars would be 299,560.

It is well to remember that if we take this latter figure of the increase of scholars as one that is reasonable, and in consequence one that reflects on the actual figure of 180,000 attained, there are certain extenuating facts to be borne in mind. It would be a gross figure, including all children, not only the church elementary school population, but also all the Roman Catholic and nonconformist children, and all those better placed pupils in the grammar and public schools. Again the National Society's figure includes only *direct* union schools, to the exclusion of all church elementary schools not in union with the society. Bearing these considerations in mind the position would seem superficially to be more satisfactory, as the number of scholars more than kept pace with the growth of population.

Public opinion, however, saw the position differently, and the National Society cannot be exonerated from the charge of " counting heads," of placing too much emphasis on mere numbers and not bothering sufficiently about the quality of the education given. It was making a gallant attempt to achieve the impossible, for it would take a very long time before the voluntary system could include all children required by contemporary standards. The raising of these standards proceeded at a higher rate than the system managed to increase its absorption of pupils and thus the position worsened progressively. Further, the quality [2] of the education offered in the schools certainly does not seem to have been correspondingly improved. This stagnation was not, of course, a new problem and is not yet an old one.

The voluntary system was proving inadequate, but the way to a new one was not clear. Yet even if we grant the fact that the voluntary system was not satisfactory, there are certain further points to be made, and " it is unhistorical to condemn the *modus vivendi* of one period because at a later one a different course is adopted." The fact that the voluntary system failed to be accepted as permanent does not diminish its value for its age,[3] and the church tried manfully to make it succeed. What the difficulties, or even misrepresentations, were may be judged from the following quotations, as well as the weakness of Government policy.

An instructive commentary on the need for checks on politically inspired pronouncements on education is furnished in a report of one of Her Majesty's Inspectors.[4] He had read a petition to Parliament from Durham and Northumberland complaining of educational destitution. The report answers that " There are places in the Northern district, where every provision that a pitman could require for the education of his children has been provided for him. South Church and Blackboy schools are strictly for colliery children. I should say that these schools are receiving a greater share of attention from those clerical managers than is usual. The registers of age, attendance and progress, which have been drawn and kept by the Rev. G. H. J. Stephens, are the most complete I have ever seen. They do not furnish, however, the very least evidence that the pitmen thereabouts have one particle of determination ' *to procure for their children a good moral education* ' (words quoted from pitmen's petition italicized in *Report*). These schools would supply exactly what the petitioners profess to require, but when this ' *good moral education* ' is brought to their very doors, they do not make the slightest effort to secure it." A mass of evidence is given in support of this analysis of the true state of affairs.[5] The

Government Report for 1856–7, quoting a different Inspector dealing with Lancashire, bears similar witness. " The truth, as I believe, is that comparatively few persons in Lancashire feel any real concern to see the people at large educated. A few persons make a good deal of noise on the subject; and a still fewer number carry on the work liberally and zealously without talk and noise; but the mass of persons are still hostile, or at best indifferent on the matter. *A public feeling for education has yet to be created.* (Italics quoted.) In saying this, however, I am bound in truth to except one class of persons from the assertion, I mean the clergy. Ever since the year 1843 I have had a most extensive insight into the educational doings of the clergy, and I cannot but attribute the main educational work which has been effected in England—and that is not slight in amount—to their zeal and their labour . . ." Statements follow about the necessity of laymen's backing for education and their present apathy.[6]

In addition to this tribute to the progressive zeal of the clergy we find an inspector himself criticizing the policy of Government as reactionary.[7] We find most pathetic appeals from clergy to the inspectors that as the Committee of Council could not help poor rural schools—they did not reach the standard required for recognition—the cause of elementary education was suffering. Her Majesty's Inspector condemns the " red-tape " of his department's regulations, states roundly that the Committee of Council is defeating its own ends and is completely out of touch with the realities of agricultural parish schools.[8] This kind of criticism may well be borne in mind when we are tempted to regard the Committee of Council as the spear-head of educational progress.

It is surprising to a modern student of the subject of elementary education at this time to see how clearly religious and political considerations were recognized by contemporaries, but how rarely the most potent of all, humanly speaking, the economic factor, was recognized for what it was worth. That clerical realist, the Rev. C. Richson (1806–74),[9] states clearly that nothing " will remove the hard fact that in a very large number of instances a parent has more than enough to do to provide sufficient food and clothing for his children." For this reason Her Majesty's Inspector, who quotes Richson,[10] goes against the convictions of Richard Dawes (and the findings of the St. Asaph Diocese Committee of Inquiry on this matter, and the opinion of the Archbishop of Canterbury) that school fees should be raised to provide "self-supporting" schools. Incidentally, this would abolish Dawes' hated "eleemosynary principle." Earlier in the report [11] are given a graduated scale of fees adopted by different clergy in their schools. Clerical zeal for a system other than that prevailing went beyond the writing of letters and pamphlets. In south east Lancashire, the most populous district in England, the Rev. Charles Richson, when on the staff of Manchester Cathedral in 1851, described efforts to secure an improvement in *A Sketch of some of the Causes which, in Manchester, induced the abandonment of the Voluntary System in the support of Schools and the Introduction of the Manchester and Salford Education Bill.*[12] This work of over 100 pages was dedicated to Bishop Prince Lee, and is worthy of careful note. We have a brief summary of the efforts for the promotion of education in this area under the voluntary system to the year 1843 : the formation of the Chester Diocesan Board of Education in 1839, and the Manchester Church Education Society. (There was much pamphlet literature on the subject of elementary education by such men as Canon Clifton, J. P. Hamilton, J. Dufton, A. Watson, R. Burgess and W. Harness. On the whole, opinion favoured some such scheme as that later proposed in Dr. Hook's famous letter.) Chapter III deals with *The Rise and Progress of the Lancashire Public School Association,* which proposed the secular solution to the elementary education question. It was felt by Richson that the National Society's terms of union were a hindrance and the Bishop of Manchester asked for a relaxation, so that distinctive Church teaching was not to be required to be given to non-church children. This request was not acceded to. (It is only fair to say that in 1902 the question of appointing nonconformist assistant teachers, especially in single school areas, came up for consideration and the National Society made no demur about such appointments where they seemed desirable.) Accordingly the Dean of Manchester and Kay-Shuttleworth (and amongst others two Roman Catholic priests, who later became bishops, helped in the early stages), held a meeting in the Mayor's Parlour and collected £8,411 to promote the Manchester and Salford Bill. But this measure was too comprehensive and was ahead of its time. It would have struck a severe blow at the voluntary system before men had any vision of a really practicable alternative.

An intensive study of the history of Manchester elementary

education during the years 1800–1870 was made with great fairness by Mr. S. E. Maltby,[13] a Nonconformist. The Manchester Church Education Society had been founded in 1845, and this is his conclusion.

" The Church Education Society manifestly took a wide view of its duties, and energetically endeavoured to carry them out. To a large extent it was able to do so, as may be seen from the later reports and from the evidence submitted by the Rev. Charles Richson to the Select Committee of 1852 : but that it was unable effectively to reduce the educational destitution of Manchester will also be apparent from later chapters.[14] No corresponding local organization, with unity of purpose and executive power, existed outside the Church, and the guess may be reasonably hazarded that other denominational schools were not more adequate, for Lord John Russell's words of 1843 that 'the Church Party is in some of the manufacturing districts an almost insignificant minority' did not apply to Manchester." [15] It would be interesting to know where exactly these words did apply.

The inescapable conclusion forced on the student of this problem of educational destitution is that its solution went far beyond the bounds of practical politics until the last third of the nineteenth century was reached.

F. THE NATIONAL SOCIETY'S GREAT INQUIRY OF 1846-7

In 1846 the Committee of Council had invaded the voluntary field, when the pupil-teacher system and pension schemes for teachers were set up, but it so happens that the period of incipient state action begins just when we have a complete picture of what the church's share in the voluntary system had accomplished.

During the years 1846-7 the National Society undertook a survey of church schools.[1] Parliament voted a sum of £500 towards the cost of preparing the work, which may be regarded as a national and authoritative document. The particulars required were to be tabulated in census form by parishes arranged alphabetically under counties. A copy of the return was sent to every incumbent and few failed to respond. A separate school was reckoned where infants, girls and boys were taught separately by different teachers in their own schoolrooms. Then the schools were classified accordingly as they were affiliated to the National Society (N) or a local church board (B) or both (NB), and their categories noted—Weekday and Sunday School, Sunday and Weekday Evening, or Weekday evening only, with separate columns for boys and girls. The total of the sexes followed next, school by school, corrected by a second column designed to remove duplicate entries, as when a pupil attended weekdays only in one school and Sundays only in another. Later students of the history of elementary education who have read Dr. Hook's Letter to Bishop Thirlwall, in which he doubts the accuracy of the National Society's figures on the score of their containing duplicate entries, and have themselves been content in consequence to doubt them ever since, may see Hook's surmise disproved. Hook's doubts were, perhaps, natural in the circumstances, but to-day this survey makes a similar misapprehension inexcusable.

The particulars of school and teacher's house followed, indicating whether the premises were legally or virtually secured, unsecured, or part of the church fabric. After these came details of school maintenance. This was supplied through endowment or quasi-endowment by private benefactors, by voluntary subscriptions, children's pence or some combination of any of these. The total cost was given also of annual maintenance. As to the teachers, their emoluments were inquired into, as well as details of paid and gratuitous help. Finally comes the "Remarks" column, from which quotations have already been given to illustrate the nature of the church parish school.[2]

This is a unique survey of the interior position of the schools of early Victorian England. It fills several hundred pages, unnumbered, of a folio volume, giving a detailed and illuminating picture of probably four schools out of five, and is of real value for the historian of social as well as of strictly educational progress. It is, therefore, a great pity that such a wealth of information should have been totally neglected by later writers.

Not least important are the tabulated returns of statistics by individual counties, and the all-embracing summaries rendered separately for England and Wales, giving us a complete bird's eye view of church elementary education in 1845-6. Some figures quoted[3] will show the position in outline : they refer to England only, where the population was 14,908,769. Figures for Sunday schools are given because in many of these secular instruction was given to children and adults who could not attend at any other time, as is clear even from the 1861 survey.[4]

No impartial student can do other than stress the real contribution to the permanent work of education that this survey witnesses to : but it was not sufficient, we may admit, to meet the needs of the country.

So much for a conspectus of the whole field of church elementary education : by way of contrast we may look at the inside of a single parish school and leave the general for the particular in the school at Wigtoft in Lancashire.[5] "This is an endowed school for the poor children of the parish in reading and writing. Arithmetic, history and geography are paid for by those who learn them. The master is a very intelligent, well-informed young man, and decidedly superior to the majority of village schoolmasters. When first I visited the village school, about six weeks ago, there were forty children in regular attendance; the average number at the present time does not exceed twenty-five. At a neighbouring village last week, I found a similar falling off. In an agricultural district like this, children are found to be useful in various kinds of field work, especially at this season of the year. Bean-dropping and wool-gathering are their chief employments. A very young child, I am told, can collect half a pound of wool (worth twopence halfpenny) in a day and thus many do not appear at school during the spring, and often not until summer is nearly over. On revisiting the school I was glad to find that the plans I had recommended were adopted, so far as circumstances would allow, with some other little alterations and improvements which are owing to the interest the Master takes in his occupation. He had procured some maps, and had mounted them very neatly. The time-table I had drawn up was copied in a beautiful hand and fixed on a board. The school-room was further decorated with the Apostles' Creed, and a table of daily prayers, both fine specimens of penmanship, and executed by a friend of the Master's. This table originated in a conversation I had had with the Master, which led to his arranging a plan of progress for use in the school, so that each day of the week should have wholly, or in part, its own devotional office, all being taken from the Liturgy. He has taken pains to make the children behave quietly and reverently during prayers, and has succeeded well, having begun by setting a good example. In this respect, and indeed in the spirit which animates the religious instruction generally, many schools of high pretension are inferior to that of Wigtoft. An interval of a quarter of an hour is allowed for recreation in the midst of the morning's work. The children then stand up and sing some specified portion of the tables and so march out to play, still singing as they go. They use a tune which the master claims as his own, and which is one of the most extraordinary specimens of musical composition it has been my lot to hear. Any attempt to express it on paper in the common notation would probably puzzle a much more scientific musician than myself. The end, however, is gained : all the tables (including the weights and measures) are well known even by the younger children, who not only repeated them correctly in order, but—what surprised me more—answered readily the questions I asked them in cross-examination. A very short space of time is devoted to this exercise—perhaps not more than five minutes each day : it amuses the children, and reconciles them to what is usually considered a very dry and uninteresting study. No music was taught in school (except the original melody already mentioned) until I introduced a few chants, which I hope will continue to be practised. The master has not passed through a Training Institution." This report is here quoted because it pictures not only a church school very vividly—the single untrained teacher almost pathetically keen to learn or to please, the spasmodic school attendance, and the lack of any system save that devised by the teacher himself, but, what is more important for our immediate purpose, it shows us, at a time when the views of the diocesan inspectors of schools were largely decisive in influencing the teacher, what were the ideals of church schools. Quite clearly in the eyes of this inspector the direct inculcation of religious instruction was of more importance than the evolution by experiment of an improved technique of secular instruction. And this was regardless of the fact that the primary work of the teacher was not to teach in the sphere more specifically reserved for the clergy. There are, indeed, signs of a tension between teachers and clergy, as from the nature of the case there was bound to be when the practitioner of teaching was entirely under the control of an *ex officio* superior with no necessary knowledge of the subject.[6] There were, indeed, real clerical pioneers of educational progress like W. L. Rham of Winkfield and Richard Dawes of King's Somborne, but the impression one cannot escape is that the control of the school by the parson occasionally became a source of dissatisfaction to some of the most spirited teachers.[7] Then the church's insistence on dogmatic teaching in the parish schools produced the charge that her interest in elementary education was far from disinterested. It was for this reason that much clerical zeal was discounted and the Committee of Council in framing regulations for school management aimed (save in the case of Roman Catholic schools) at creating a strong lay element. English people seem instinctively to have felt that the church's control over education was an inconsistency and widely opposed it for this reason: "freedom" is still the most marked characteristic of English education to-day. That the National Society and some clergy at least were not out of sympathy with democratic aspirations entirely is shown by the fact that the Society's *Monthly Paper* (see next chapter) of June 30th, 1848 (No. XIX) claims that "Chartism is neither more nor less than the organized remonstrance of the working classes against the neglect and indifference with which they have been treated by those, who, in the ordinary course of affairs have profited by their labour." After a definition of education primarily as character training we get the statement that " Education is the one great panacea for all the evils of this country." " Every poor man's child is entitled to this training. How many of them get it? " These words suggest a real vision of the social value of education that has been abundantly proved in our own day. " Those who feared for their property on April 10th (1848) may rest assured that education is the best police." There has never been a truer forecast of the results of one of the most vital aspects of social amelioration in Victorian England.

G. THE WORK OF THE NATIONAL SOCIETY TO THE EVE OF THE ACT OF 1870

AFTER the great survey just mentioned the next feature in the history of the National Society is the *Monthly Paper*. First issued in 1847, it contained much matter of interest to teachers such as the professional papers now supply so abundantly. It was a medium for making known staff vacancies, advertising school appliances, and gave notes and figures relating to the progress of the National Society. Extracts from Government reports and applications for help from the society, many of them really pathetic, figure in the early issues. As time went on Examination Papers for Teachers' Certificates of Merit set by the Government inspectors, lesson notes on various subjects, e.g. an object lesson on " Coal," and answers to correspondents all appear. But in addition to these items this pioneer of scholastic journalism, open as it was to correspondents and outside contributors, became less " official " than the annual reports of the society and contained opinions expressed on current educational topics and wider sociological issues.[1]

In 1848 the Harvest Lectures became noteworthy. These were " refresher courses " for teachers and conferences for the interchange of ideas, and resembled the modern Easter activities of teachers. Incidentally the title " Harvest Lectures " illustrates the close connexion between farm activities and children's attendance at school.[2]

In 1845 also the Depository of the National Society was opened for the sale of books and educational materials of all kinds. The Committee of Council merely published a list of recommended books, similar to the " permitted " list of the L.C.C. to-day. Unfortunately two schools of thought grew up with the result that their differences became more acute, and the parties bought from the list of the Committee of Council or from the National Society according to their preconceived ideas, regardless of considerations of merit or progress.[3] But much good work was done by this pioneer effort in mass publishing and retailing of elementary school books, and sales rose by approximately £1,000 per annum in the years 1845–8 to £6,365.[4] The Registry of Teachers available for employment began in 1859.[5]

The years 1856–7—the state Education Department was set up in Feb., 1856—conclude another decennium and a further statistical survey is produced by the National Society. This, however, is on a much smaller scale than the monumental work of 1846–7, nor are strict comparisons possible, save in a few respects, between the statistics of these surveys.[6]

" A large proportion of the returns show a great deficiency in the school funds, which in many cases has to be supplied by the clergyman—a deficiency which often amounts to an annual sum of £20, £30, £40 or even more." [7]

It appears that the increase during the last ten years in the number of children under instruction in the church schools has more than kept pace with the increase of the population. " This fact cannot but be regarded as highly satisfactory and encouraging," the National Society claimed. Taking England, Wales, the Isle of Man, and the Channel Islands the percentages of the population in church schools are as below : (p. iii).

1837	1847	1857
6·65	8·259	8·611
= 1 in 15	= 1 in 12½	= 1 in 11½

These figures are crude, and give no idea of the numbers of children in the various age groups, and on the most vital point, that of quality, we have no guidance. On such facts (p. viii) as (a) scholars' ages, (b) subjects of instruction, (c) average number of days per annum attended by each scholar, (d) number of certificated teachers, (e) number of schools under diocesan inspection, (f) number of schools in which industrial instruction is given, no details were required. This was due to a desire to simplify things in the interests of managers.

The figures given below show the difficulties that the schools had to face. A survey was made of the numbers of children in seven Manchester parishes.

Children attending in some day school	4,779	
Children at home, but attending day schools like the rest at convenient periods	3,619	
		8,398
Children at work	1,448	
Children not attending any day school	1,289	
		2,737
		11,135

" It is important to notice in the above return that 8,398
children were connected with some existing schools, whether
public or private, though only 4,779 children were in actual
daily attendance; and hence the fallacy is apparent of
estimating how many children are receiving education from
the average number of children in daily attendance at
school." [8]

There was a great increase of facilities, provided by the
National Society from its Special Fund of £150,000 raised
in 1843–5. The survey (p. iv) states that " a great part of
the work of bringing the children of the labouring classes
under instruction had been accomplished between 1837–47
and a proportionately great increase could not be expected
in the following decade."

" The number of scholars in Church Evening Schools in
1847 was 22,558, or ·131% of the population; in 1857 it
was 54,157, or ·279%" (pp. v and vi).[9]

" It appears from the returns made under the Educational
Census of 1851, by Mr. Horace Mann, that in that year there
were 935,892 scholars in Church Sunday Schools. The
Society's inquiry shows that the number of scholars in such
schools in 1857 was 1,093,070, and that of this number
661,868 attended weekday schools also." This means that if
413,202 attended on Sundays only the fault was not neces-
sarily that of the church, or of the parents.

We learn (p. ii) that " It appears that during the last ten
years there has been a marked diminution in the number of
dames' schools, owing no doubt to the very great increase in
the number of National schools, though mainly perhaps to
the improved methods of instruction which have been adopted
in existing parochial schools." This is a real sign of progress,
in that by the reverse action of a sort of scholastic Gresham's
Law the better schools were driving out the worse.[10]

" During the last ten years there has been a steady increase
in the number of legally secured schoolrooms and teachers'
residences, also in the number of teachers, assistant teachers,
pupil teachers and paid monitors." [11]

Turning to the financial aspect of elementary education,
we might be tempted to adopt an unfair criterion and
minimize the cash expenditure of £656,916 per annum. But
this sum represents only sums " returned," and compared
with the state grant of £629,056 it gives Churchmen no
cause for shame. On page viii of the survey we are told that

in each diocese " An attempt has been made to estimate the average annual income of each weekday school, and the average cost per annum of each weekday scholar. These estimates, it will be seen, vary somewhat in the several counties, and it is evident that they are considerably below the sums actually received and expended for the purposes of Church Education. For example, by sifting the numbers it appears that the average annual cost of the education of each weekday scholar throughout England and Wales, the Isle of Man and the Channel Isles is 11/4d., a sum which, being calculated from very defective returns as regards income, must be far short of the case." Actual tests of schools in mining, manufacturing and agricultural districts show that a little over 15/- is an under-estimate.

The clergy manifested real concern over the question of those who left school early to engage in manual labour:[12] the rise in the number of evening schools is partly due to this concern. This problem of moral and religious welfare is still acute, and there are instances of individual after-care work, in a single small area, apart from the evening schools.

The vicar of Whitkirk and his wife organized a music class, a class for colliers, and a library.[13] Nearby in Leeds itself was a Factory Girls' Sewing School with a nightly attendance of between 90 and 130 girls and women.[14] At Harewood, close by, there was a Literary and Scientific Institution that anticipated the activities of the W.E.A. and the County Library.[15]

The aim of moral and religious education is to provide the armour of salvation. Many lists could be compiled showing the material value of the education received in church elementary schools, as, for example, the list of " Old Scholars " of parish schools and their success in bettering themselves given by Her Majesty's Inspectors in 1863-4,[16] or in a previous year's report,[17] where the good results of moral training are given. Only 11 girls out of a total of 397 whose after-school careers were investigated very carefully some years later " have subsequently forfeited their good name." The clergy's insistence on religious teaching was based on the assumption that the lessons of early life imprinted an indelible mark on the child's character. And the fact that children were not always responsive to questioning on the catechism, that they found it impossible often to express their lessons in theological language and were generally inarticulate on religious matters does not imply by any means that they missed the value of these lessons. The following quotation from one of Her Majesty's Inspector's reports [18] represents the replies of a boy of eleven years of age, living on the banks of the Thames. The inspector thinks " they might be profitably adopted by many persons of riper years, and of more exalted station."

" Tell me of any state of life to which it may, perhaps, please God to call you."

" A Waterman."

" Well, how would you do your duty in that state? "

" Take no more passengers than the licence says."

" Well, anything besides? "

" Behave civil to the passengers."

" Anything else? "

" *Land 'em dry on the other side.*"   (Italics quoted.)

" Anything else? "

" Ask no more than the regular fare."

" Anything else? "

" Keep some of the money for my father and mother."

" Anything more? "

" Try to lead a good life."

" I have heard in my time more lengthy and less complete commentaries on ' your duty towards your neighbour,' than ' undertaking no more than your boat will carry—claiming no more than the regular fare—and landing them dry on the other side.' "

In the Sunday schools there is a marked decrease—coincident, be it noted, with their decline as centres of secular teaching—in the number of paid teachers in favour of voluntary helpers.

To return to the more domestic progress of the National Society: we notice that in 1860 [19] exhibitions for teachers at training institutions were set up, half of the grant being paid by the local diocesan board and half by the society. On the same basis, the society with the boards made grants to schools for books, and in this way £1,100 was expended. [20] Organizing masters to encourage and help in the schools were busy in five dioceses. [21]

Next year, in 1861, Teachers' Aid Grants were made to local boards, and the committee views with approval the growth of night schools, offers to help in paying Organizing Masters (although the growth of a body of trained teachers caused a fall in the demand for these experts) and in any other way possible.

The year 1861 is notable as the Jubilee of the National Society and in the Statistical Appendix to the present work is a brief summary of its achievements during the half-century.[22]

The sales from the Westminster depot were £190,000. It may be well to note that not more than 10,000 of the schools are under the Committee of Council's inspection. That is, about half of the number were ineligible for Government grants and were not included in state statistics. School building grants of the Privy Council were reduced to nearly 50% of the amounts given two or three years before, and there was every reason to fear the reduction of similar state grants to training schools, for the supply of school books, etc. But the society still had a wide field open to it, it was claimed, in the need for a supply of books, materials and apparatus, in helping small parish schools, in assisting managers of schools to obtain certificated teachers, to establish night schools, to prepare " teachers specially adapted for schools in rural parishes which scarcely require the services of a master or mistress sent out from a training institution." This does not indicate a desire to lower the standard of rural teaching any more than in the employment of uncertificated teachers to-day, but it does show that attempts were being made to avoid the imposition of an impossible financial burden on local voluntary effort in poor parishes. Finally, it was claimed that the Society had by its vigilance done good service to the cause of church education where its interests were threatened or overlooked and that it behoved the Church of England to have some central body which would resist attempts to secularize education. The Appendix is signed by the Archbishop of Canterbury (J. B. Sumner).

Continuing the story of National Society expansion, we may note [23] that the turn-over of the Depository in its first year was £3,130, but in the last fifteen months (1864–5) its figure was £34,878. This vast sum is evidence of a most extensive effort to equip schools with what the Society considered the best books and apparatus.

A novel feature is that Middle or Commercial Schools may be received into connexion with the National Society or diocesan boards provided that they give church teaching and that the schools will be open to the occasional visitations of the clergy.

In the 1866 *Annual Report* [24] reference is made to further statistics, and in *A Letter to His Grace the Archbishop of Canterbury* headed "*Do our National Society Schools provide education for all whom they ought to train?*" *by the Revd. Robert Gregory, M.A.* (1865), we meet the following claim :

Of the 795,571 children in church schools that received Government grants in 1864, only 13,841 paid more than 4d. per week, but in 1855 the children numbered 364,227 (the dissenters' figures are stated to be 10,404 and the Roman Catholics' 291), of whom 9,169 were paying more than 4d. per week. That is, the National Society brought the benefits of cheap elementary education to a hugely increased number of children and this under Government inspection, of whom a vastly decreased number paid 4d. or more per week per head. These figures are said to mean that of the 430,000 children now added to the numbers in church schools only 4,600 belonged to any section of the " middle class " : the " lower class " percentage increase was 118, but the " middle class " percentage increase was 51.

The Royal Commissioners of 1858 had claimed that there were 11,024 " parishes " without a school and the National Society in 1867 faced this charge. [25] Now the word " parish " may be ambiguous : it may be the unit of ecclesiastical organization, centring round church and parson, along the lines of which the church planned her provision of schools, or it may refer to that legal fiction, the " civil parish." The commissioners give a very misleading picture of " educational destitution." There were 14,877 civil parishes, and that is over 11,114 more than the number of ecclesiastical parishes. Again, 405 ecclesiastical parishes have 5 houses or under. Further, endowed and independent schools, largely satisfactory to the church as giving her teaching, are for this purpose left out of the reckoning. Wealthy landowners set up schools, yet sometimes they refused the offer of visits by H.M. Inspectors, and private schools existed, helped by the clergy. Finally, the implied suggestion that every parish needed a school was nonsensical : e.g. Norwich with its 36 parishes certainly did not need 36 schools. These points must, in fairness to the church, be made, since official records provide the main sources of information for students of the history of education and are apt to be misleading.

But the cry of " educational destitution " was ominous for the National Society and the decennial survey of 1866–7 is chiefly concerned to defend the church's work for voluntary education against its critics.[26]

The *Statistics of Church of England Schools for the Poor in England and Wales for the years 1866 and 1867* (2nd Edn. 50 pp. 1/-) is of considerable importance. Not only does it go into far greater detail than the previous reckoning, but it is also a more business-like document in every way, relating its figures, quoted in the Statistical Appendix, more closely to the facts of school life. In addition, it gives us a final picture of what the Church of England had accomplished almost at the end of the *ancien régime*—before the state displaced the church as the dominant factor in English elementary education.

Finally, here is a picture of the sort of school under the voluntary system which made people at least desire some form of state control. Mr. Dicker acted as an organizing master under Miss Burdett-Coutts' [27] scheme to a group of six schools in Devonshire, all under clerical control. His answers show that the largest school had 116 children : the smallest, 14. He gives particulars of the distance the children had to walk to school : in one case tolls had to be paid. Some of the schools were inspected by H.M. Inspectors, some not. Children pay from one penny to threepence per week : at Shaldon, children who write pay from twopence to threepence, and others from a penny to twopence. The children's ages range from three to eight years, with boys and girls present in about equal numbers. At Barton (28 pupils): "Only about 15 over six years of age. Two or three babies attend with their sisters. N.B. If these babies were not allowed to come, their sisters could not attend."

Mr. Forster cast his shadow before him : the annual report of the National Society for the year 1868 [28] has an appendix containing a short petition against the state education bill before the House of Commons, and a memorandum was transmitted to the Lord President of the Council against the iniquitous system of " payment by results " introduced under the Revised Code by Lowe.[29] This was especially regarded as unfair to poor rural schools, who were discriminated against because they could not afford certificated teachers. Bureaucracy under Lowe did the cause of popular education real disservice, but the faithful were not forgetful of their cause and the necessity of standing up to the obscurantism of the Government and the apathy of the people. And it is interesting to note that in the years 1815–1868 legacies to the National Society ranged from £1 1s. to £18,000.[30]

The first *Report of the Middle-class Schools Committee* appeared in 1869.[31] The people whom it was proposed to help were the foremen and small employers, clerks, farmers, and superior artisans. It is pointed out that these are bound to enter private schools, " the general character of which is known to all interested in education." In answer to a circular which was sent out, £2,234 was promised, with annual subscriptions of £261. Grants for eight places were made and a trust-deed drawn up for such schools. Local examinations for all schools will be held simultaneously in December. But the main concern of the National Society is the topic of " educational destitution." [32] The Committee took the view that rate-aided and compulsory education would never be acceptable or even be workable, and quoted the Prince Consort to that effect. (But the tide had flowed more swiftly than they knew since His Royal Highness delivered himself of prophecy in 1857.)

It does happen that by chance there is an official church pronouncement on the question of educational destitution under the voluntary system in 1870—by the Lower House of Convocation of the Province of Canterbury.[33] Quoting an earlier report by the York House, they show clearly that there were great discrepancies in the estimates of destitution by reliable authorities. Further, the *Report* shows clearly the misleading character of the Committee of Council's statistics. We may say now that any one reading the annual reports, particularly where a distinction is drawn between sums paid to schools inspected and not inspected respectively, may naturally assume that the committee's figures take cognizance of all public elementary schools: there is nowhere a specific indication to the contrary.[34]

The Canterbury report (p. 12) says that " . . . 5,656 Church schools must be added to the Committee of Council's returns,"

Inspected Schools	9,894
Uninspected Schools	5,656
Total	15,550

and this excludes uninspected schools belonging to other bodies, but all going to fill the picture of achievement under the voluntary system (p. 16). " It must be remembered that in Church of England Schools, not aided by the State, there were in 1866 609,168 scholars on the registers, and 413,523 in average attendance. Assuming that the amount expended upon education in these schools to be not less than the amount locally raised in State-aided schools we must add to the above a further sum of not less than £498,000. Besides the building and support of Elementary Schools, the Church of England has also provided by voluntary subscriptions for the building of Normal Schools, and their appurtenances, £194,085 to meet Parliamentary Grants amounting to £91,474. During the year 1868, for the maintenance of these colleges and students, £16,613 was contributed from all sources (including students' fees) to meet Government Grants amounting to £41,530. It thus appears that the amount provided by the Church of England in the year 1868 (exclusive of Government Grants) was :—

In support of Normal (State-aided) Schools				£16,613
„	„	„	Elementary „ „ „	664,270
„	„	„	Other Schools, not less than	498,000
			Total (in one year)	£1,178,883

It should be remembered, too, that this has been and probably is a steadily increasing sum." The annual state grant in 1869 for primary schools was only £415,000.[35]

Attempts have been made to minimize the zeal of church-men for national elementary education, but the fact that in one year they cared exactly £1,178,883 worth of sympathy takes a deal of explaining away.

H. PIONEER VILLAGE SCHOOLS AND SIMILAR EFFORTS

IT is now time to study a department of the clergy's educational achievement, sharply contrasted with the mass effort of the National Society. Individual clergy tried to find by pioneer experiment their own solution to the problem of the parish or urban school. Here at once the work of the Revd. Richard Dawes[1] is outstanding. For seventeen years a don at Cambridge, he went to his parish of King's Somborne with no experience of elementary education. Dawes' educational creed may be summarized as follows:

(a) The poor will only set a value on schooling that is really efficient.
(b) A great amount of social amelioration results from an extension of the secular education of the poor.
(c) The good school will tend to support itself.

Her Majesty's Inspector thought highly of Dawes' work:[2] "In one of the schools of my district an educational experiment has for the last five years been trying, which has excited so much of the public attention, and has been attended with results, a knowledge of which appears to me of so much importance to the progress of education, that it claims a special notice at my hands." He further states that Dawes' own *Suggestive Hints,* from which we shall quote, "ought to be in the hands of every elementary teacher."

The schools at King's Somborne were opened by Dawes in Oct., 1842: they cost about £600, provided by "liberal assistance from the Committee of Council, the National Society, the Diocesan Board of Winchester, and by subscriptions from myself and others connected with the property of the parish."[3] There were originally 38 children. The following tables show the growth of numbers, increase of amounts received in fees, and increased sums spent on books for the Library, which played such an important part in the work of social and educational amelioration brought about by these schools in the parish.

Labourers paid twopence for the first and a penny for each additional child per week. The initial apathy of the parents

was changed, and by 1847 one seventh of the resident population of King's Somborne was being educated in the parish
schools.[4] Dawes offers a severe criticism of " the eleemosynary
principle," and claims that it does not appeal to the motive
of self-sacrifice on the part of the parents of poor children.
His own district was not exceptional : " Here in a district
where the rate of wages is at least as low as in others, and
where, if the people be not as poor, it must be due to the
operation of moral causes, he finds a self-supporting school,
having more than the usual staff of teachers, adequately
paid."[5]

Payment of school fees was strictly insisted upon, and more
than 8/9 of the numbers on the books are in daily attendance.
We may note that the average income of a labourer was nine
shillings per week and a boy may earn from one-and-six to
half-a-crown a week. Yet of *labourers' children* there were
five boys over fourteen and nine over twelve, and eleven
girls over thirteen, of whom eight were over fourteen years
of age.

It is, perhaps, typical of the state of small local charities
that an annual sum of £8 left as an educational endowment
in the parish could not be obtained for the use of Dawes'
schools.[6]

Those above the labouring class who lived in the parish
paid 6/- per quarter : if living outside, 10/- per quarter.

In 1842 there were   38 children.
  „ 1843 „   „   106   „
  „ 1844 „   „   110   „
  „ 1845 „   „   144   „
  „ 1846 „   „   158   „   of whom 36 paid by the
quarter, and 14 were from outside the parish.

In 1850 there were 219 children. Of these, 31 (27 boys, 4
girls) paid 10/- per quarter, and 24 (11 boys, 13 girls) paid
6/- per quarter. There were 112 (52 boys, 60 girls) " pence
children."[7] In addition, there were 52 children in the Junior
School who paid 2d. per week, and as a sort of preparatory
school the Dame School was now flourishing.

A note on the organization of the school may help to show
one factor in Dawes' success. In addition to charging comparatively high fees—and the National Society had always
thought that people value something more if they pay for
it—the teachers were well paid : master and mistress (man

and wife) receive £70 with house and garden, and the second master (an "old boy" of 17) £25, raised to £30. There were four paid monitors, later superseded by pupil-teachers.[8]

But Dawes was a parish priest as well as a pioneer educationist: "Mr. Dawes conceived the idea of working out, within the walls of his school, a moral reformation in his parish," previously much demoralized by the Poor Law. We may refer to the section of the Committee of Council's 1847–8 *Report*, Appendix,[9] "Influence of the King's Somborne School on the moral condition of the Parish," from which the words quoted above are taken.

The stories about the happenings in the parish occasioned by Dawes, of the parish's decline in drunkenness, its decency and cleanliness, a virtual reformation, are truly affecting. We may cite the case of the little girl who gave a not too bright reply to the question of a visiting Lady Bountiful (doubtful as to whether these beautifully tidied children were indeed those of village labourers), and was asked what her head was for. The child curtsied and replied, "To comb, ma'am." Possibly one or two quotations[10] may make Dawes' work more real. Children took home evening work in their satchels, with books borrowed from the library: "Another father said, 'Ask to keep the book longer, as I want to hear the last out.' And the mother of this child has told me more than once, speaking of her husband, who had been addicted to drinking, that he was quite a changed man, which she entirely attributed to the great interest he took in the school occupation of his children, and in their making his evenings happy at home. In this cottage I find a map of the two hemispheres and of Europe, very small, given them by a neighbour: and it seems the father has a particular fancy in tracing out all the places he hears his children read of. One child, a girl about 13 years of age, to whom *Mutiny on the Bounty* was lent, was found by the master the other day, at the dinner hour, standing on a stool before a map of the world, and tracing out the places the ship had touched at."

Then there was the girl of 15, who came from a very unsatisfactory home, who taught herself the very rudiments and then sat among the little children and rose to the top class. She saved a shilling to buy the *Fourth Lesson Book*, which she bought at once, because when she required it she might not have the money. She placed what best clothes she had in a box and "drew them up to the roof of the cottage to keep them out of the dirt."

Richard Dawes realized that a real education was indeed a panacea for the ills of society. " I have often when inclined to pass very severe censures on the beer house and other degrading amusements to which the agricultural labourers are addicted, felt myself checked by the consideration that totally uneducated as they are, they were not capable of any other enjoyment than those of a sensual nature, and that, humanly speaking, it was almost impossible with the generation already grown up, to effect much good, excepting through their children." [11]

In return for his services to the cause of popular education Lord John Russell presented Dawes to the Deanery of Hereford, but after his departure the schools prospered, on the testimony of the new incumbent, owing to the soundness of their foundation work.[12] More, the King's Somborne Schools became models for other parishes: [13] e.g. at Abbot's Ann, Hants, where the school was so popular that as many as eleven children walked eleven miles, out and home, per day. Many children became weekly boarders in the local cottages,[14] as they lived too far distant to be regular attenders otherwise at Dawes' and other schools. At Stockbridge, in some schools in Winchester, at Wellow, Downham Market (Norfolk), Woodhill (Herts), Much Marcle (Hereford), Sudbury, Acton (Cheshire), Stone (Staffs), St. Thomas's Schools, Charterhouse, Tamworth Charity Schools, Alverstoke, and many others Dawes' methods were copied. Later, as Dean, Dawes did much good work at the Hereford Bluecoat School and the Ledbury National Schools.

After studying these efforts to create a new type of village school we may now proceed to examine a complimentary enterprise for the town poor. Details of the schools at St. Thomas's, Charterhouse are most conveniently seen in the Committee of Council's *Report* of 1856–7 : [15] these are very good schools set up amid very adverse conditions. " The clerical income, after paying curate and expenses, is less than £200 per annum, without a residence ; but by great exertions and self-sacrifice, combined with unusual talent in founding, organizing, and managing schools, the incumbent has provided for the educational needs of his district to an extent, which, under the most favourable circumstances, has scarcely been equalled in any parish of this Metropolis." In the following year we meet the statement that [16] " the schools . . . have cost £19,031 within the last few years. They are

neat, well-built and well-arranged, but there are no super-
fluities of building or decoration . . . There are no opulent
residents, and this large sum has been raised by the personal
exertions of the clergyman, the Rev. W. Rogers,[17] and by
the liberality of the Government and Mr. Rogers's own
friends." (Our italics.) The details noted may indicate the
nature and extent of the work done in these schools.[18]

But there was both in town and country an attempt to
bridge the gap between income and expenditure by raising
fees. The aim was not so much to save the pockets of
possible subscribers, but to waive the "eleemosynary
principle," on the ground that a school really benefited by
being financially independent. There must be added self-
sacrifice, they themselves were to pay for their own education.
"Self-supporting" schools became the cry, and lists of such
schools are not uncommon: cf. the sermon of one of Her
Majesty's Inspectors, the Rev. H. W. Bellairs.[19]

One way in which schools in the countryside could help
themselves to be more nearly economically self-supporting
was to grow market garden produce or even to engage in
genuine small-holding enterprises.[20] Apart from the money
aspect, such schools did not lend themselves to the charge
that education made the country boy dissatisfied with his lot
on the land. We may cite the following examples of these
schools: the "Industrial Gardens" at Elsecar village school,[21]
the Winkfield School of Industry,[22] Ockham, Crowborough,
Willingdon, and others,[23] all of which receive good reports
from Her Majesty's Inspectors.

The Rev. W. L. Rham (1778–1843),[24] "the benevolent
originator of this institution, . . . so well known as an
accomplished agriculturalist," had begun at Winkfield and in
1843 had 50 boys and 50 girls—very large numbers in his
day—and over two acres were intensively cultivated. In
addition, the boys had a little workshop experience. The
girls had appropriate work to do, and the great improvement
in manners and intelligence brought the pupils into great
demand. The Committee of Management was very diligent
and £21 was distributed at the year end among the pupils
to provide clothes and necessaries. The actual schooling,
however, was weak and shows Rham's work to be provisional:
it was only a step towards the normal parish school, even if it
did contain elements of real and permanent value.

The 1930's have seen a remarkable development of the

school medical services, the provision of meals and the " milk in schools" scheme, all of which have had really beneficial results. Yet as early as the first half of the last century we have a similar bold experiment in the " Feeding Schools." [25] In 1849 the Honourable and Reverend Grantham Yorke, rector of St. Philip's, Birmingham—finding that in his parish there was a large number of persons not only too poor to send their children to an ordinary school but even too poor to provide them with proper food whilst in attendance at school —opened a school for the children of parents not absolutely paupers, but who were still too poor to pay even twopence a week. This school was entirely free. It soon became popular : and, by the aid of benevolent persons, Mr. Yorke was enabled to erect a suitable building, which had from time to time been considerably enlarged, and in which the school was now carried on, its plan having been so far modified as to admit a considerable number of inmates, many of whom were orphans of soldiers killed in the late (Crimean) War.   There were 106 inmates, who were fed, lodged and clothed, a stipulated payment being annually made by their friends, or by persons who took an interest in them. There were also 130 day scholars, of whom 50, on five days weekly, received two meals at the school—dinner and supper ; in return for which they were expected to work for a given time, the boys in the tailor's or shoemaker's shop, and the girls at sewing.

Exactly what this school could mean in terms of human values the following extract may show.   " I recollect hearing the case of a girl, about eleven years old, who was in the ' feeding ' class ; when the time came for her to attend school, her mother—a widow—cried bitterly because she was obliged to send the child away without food.   ' Never mind, mother,' said the courageous girl, ' I am not *very* (italics quoted) hungry.   I can keep up till one o'clock : and I shall get some dinner then.' "   It is worth while referring to the appendix, showing the " Birmingham Industrial School Dietary Time Table," and the footnote :   " The children take their baths every week." [26]

The effect of the " feeding " on both school attendance and length of school life are sufficiently striking for us to wonder why this point was not discussed by contemporary writers.   The average age of the " feeding " class was ten years :   of the other day scholars only seven years eleven months.   The respective figures for attendance are 91% and

65%. Many little hands must have blessed the Hon. and Rev. Grantham Yorke.

Some remarks may be made on *The plan of Juvenile Labour and Adult Education adopted in the Writer's Manufactory,* by Edward Akroyd, M.P. for Huddersfield.[27] Akroyd was a convinced churchman—he says so—and pays tribute to the help given him in his work, which in some ways resembled that of Sir Titus Salt at Saltaire, by two neighbouring incumbents, the Rev. C. R. Holmes and the Rev. J. Hope.

There was an infant school for 380 children between the ages of three and eight years, who each paid twopence per week. As many as 1,000 children between eight and thirteen, all connected with the Akroyd works, and 110 others having no connexion and coming from outside, attended the Factory School. In addition to all this, there was a Working man's college, divided into senior and junior departments, catering for the age groups 13–18 years and 18 plus years respectively. This enterprise had 150 students, whilst the young women had various organized evening cultural and educational activities for 160 of their number. There were allotments for the gardeners, recreation ground and organized club games. The grand total of persons taking part in the various works for educating the people was 1,800 and the religious teaching was not specifically that of the church, so that all should feel at home.

A pious foundation of an ancient type, Henshaw's Blue Coat School, Oldham, was founded in 1834 for poor boys of 8–11 years and is still a church school, recognized by the Board of Education.[28] By way of comparison, the Rev. Desmond Morse-Boycott's St. Mary of the Angels Choir School [29] trains elementary school boys along new lines for an ordination course. Rowancroft School, Exeter,[30] trains elementary school boys of 13–14 years, giving them a good secondary boarding school education as a preparation for a course leading to ordination or the mission field. These instances are given to show the unity between to-day and the period of a hundred years ago in the life of the church.

As a general rule the countryside activities of schools were successful: similarly, the "industrial" work carried on in connexion with day schools was a failure.[31] In this context, we refer to simple day schools carrying on work along the lines of "home industry," local crafts, and selling (where possible) the finished product.

Then there were the "half-time" schools for young men and boys engaged part of their time in factory or mill. For them it was a case of part-time schooling or none at all, for their parents took them away to do a job of work. Finally, we have the state Industrial (now Home Office Approved) Schools, who received their inmates on a magistrate's commital order : with them we have no concern.

At Saltney, in Cheshire, there were girls' industrial schools,[32] offering a complete system of domestic training. The managers of the Christ Church, Albany St., Schools rented premises for a cookery school. The industrial department of St. Philip's, Hulme undertook cooking, washing and sewing.[33]

There were half-time church schools at, amongst many other places, Acton, Ellesmere,[34] Tarporley, formed to keep a hold on children who left school at too young an age. The school at Rostherne was notable and we have a report on five years of its work. The Acton school seemed to have combined the features of "half-time," industrial school and allotment gardens, and we may therefore notice it in some slight detail.[35]

About 20 boys worked on the neighbouring farms or in the Hall gardens at 3d. per half-day, whilst 30–40 others were in training for this half-time class. Work was found in a household large enough to show clearly the value of routine, for some 30 of the elder girls in rotation. The figures for attendance are said to be above the average, and nearly all the children stayed for between 5–6 years. The average age of the boys was 13 years ; of the girls, 12–10 years. It is remarkable that the merit capitation grant from the Treasury was received for 150 of the 270 pupils.[36]

Mr. Day of Ellesmere, whom we shall notice later, organized a "national school half-day labour class" for the poorer boys.[37] The "self-supporting" ideal has much to be said for it, but we notice a "free school" at Charterhouse.[38] Here is another instance and the proper explanation. "Of one thing my experience renders me sure, viz., that in all great towns there is a large residuum of extremely poor persons, for whom it is absolutely necessary that free schools should be provided if the children are to receive any continuous education. In the district of St. Philip's, Hulme,[39] in Manchester, which is better cared for than most others, this matter is specially and generously attended to. In addition to providing large boys' and girls' schools, and two infant

schools, the managers of the schools have provided a free
school for the education of those necessitous poor who are
always found in considerable numbers, living from hand to
mouth in the most unhealthy courts and alleys of towns like
Manchester and Liverpool." [40]

Pioneer work of another kind was done at Harrow Weald
by the Rev. E. Munro, author of *Agricultural Colleges*.
His plan was to help the " school-leavers," the plough-boys
and farm lads, by making it possible for them to live together
in groups or communities. Eighteen labourers, aged fourteen
to eighteen, found for the first time cleanliness, decency and
privacy in a cottage " hostel " specially fitted up as a contrast
to the crowded conditions of contemporary cottage life.[41]

A further venture of faith, a daring experiment, was
St. John's College, Ellesmere. The vicar built a room for
60 boys. He hired a house so that 14 of his pupils could
reside in this " college " with their teacher, Mr. Jones. (The
nominal village teacher was incompetent but irremovable, so
his own pupils taught in the school, leaving the teacher to
enjoy his salary.) Mr. Day published the accounts of his
college, showing how a charge of £20—the fee at the York
and Ripon Diocesan Training College—would keep the
institution going. The accounts are *pro forma*, since Mr.
Day paid for some of the pupils entirely himself : he naïvely
wishes to defend his figures and says that this is nobody's
affair save his own. No external help was required, although
the squire did give them £20 to visit the Great Exhibition
of 1851.[42]

In the *Report* of the Committee of Council for 1878-9 [43]
there is a tribute to the late Canon Fry, who " continued to
the last his self-imposed services in the cause of education "
and died at the age of 86. Here are some notes on this
" pioneer in the cause of education," written by a former
student of his who took Orders.[44] " His first aim was to
educate the schoolmasters and the schoolmistresses. With a
view to this, he set apart a room in his own house at Leicester,
in which he gathered a good number of girls and youths to
whose education he devoted himself, spending daily about
seven or eight hours in their education. The youths were
mainly educated in Mathematics and Latin ; the girls through
English grammar, religious knowledge and arithmetic. Canon
Fry's aim was to strengthen and evolve the powers of the mind
rather than to store with various kinds of knowledge. Many of

the best of the youths taught by him were sent to St. Mark's College, of which he was a warm supporter. In addition to these younger people he had under him older ones whom he sent directly to village schools, as masters and mistresses, after a period of tuition and practising in one of the Leicester schools. On Saturdays a good number of acting schoolmasters were gathered into his study, and they devoted the day to their own mental improvement under his direction. During the harvest holidays there was a larger gathering of schoolmasters and mistresses in Leicester, and an organizing master or one of his old pupils who had been to a Training College was engaged by Canon Fry to superintend their instruction, which on these occasions took a somewhat wider range than that above-mentioned. Later on in life, Canon Fry devoted himself to the increase of elementary schools, and he was one of the first members of the Leicester School Board."

Somewhat similar work was done at Lincoln, where the night schools of the chancellor (E. W. Benson, later Archbishop of Canterbury) [45] were a social club offering a training in hobbies as well as in the secular instruction of the day school. In Chancellor Leeke's time [46] in 1891 there was an " over 12 " day continuation school for 30 boys, with a workshop and technical instruction. This progressed rapidly and there were 90 boys in the VIIth standard or above. They were inspected and the work was allowed a Government grant. Of course much earlier work of this kind had been done: in 1848 the Rev. Wm. Short, Rector of St. George's, Bloomsbury, set up an adult school at Little Ormond Yard, where no policeman dared venture at night. (Earlier still Bishop Hinds [47] had been a real pioneer of night schools.) Parents asked for their children to be admitted and there were paid teachers for boys and girls. [48]

To-day we are seeing in peace time the Cambridge village colleges and in war camp schools for elementary school children who have been moved by the Government. The Rev. J. C. Cox produced an anticipation of these in 1850: *Plea for Parochial Boarding Schools*. [49] This is full of sound educational ideals, e.g. the necessity of good food, of exercise, tidy clothes and a fitting environment. But his boarding school scheme must surely be unique: he would extend resident schooling to the poor, and the more the poverty, the greater the need. Such a scheme at St. George's, Bloomsbury is quoted, which drew 75 boarders from the extreme poor. The cost is to be met by fees, local subscriptions, benefactions and endowments, grants from church societies and a Government tax. It is quite possible that if it had seen the light the resources of Victorian England could have fulfilled Cox's dream.

No man will ever know what the clergy did in their parishes for popular education: only occasionally is the veil lifted and by chance a man's work revealed, of which otherwise we should know nothing, as when Sir. A. H. Elton [50] before the Newcastle Commissioners pays tribute to the great zeal for education and allied ability of his late friend, the Rev. Thos. Wolley. "No attempt has ever been made to estimate the vast sums spent by the clergy of the Revival in building and re-building the Elementary Schools in their parishes, but many like Canon C. E. Brooke spent themselves and their fortunes on such work." [51]

Of men who seem to tower above their contemporaries yet spend their lives on simple things we may mention Canon Rawnsley,[52] already honoured as a poet and for his work for the National Trust. Yet his work for education is truly memorable. A pupil of Thring, a fellow-navvy with Lord Milner under foreman Ruskin at Hinksey, as an undergraduate he wrote: "If ever it were my lot to teach children or to manage a national school, I would interest them in the things of nature daily around them . . . 'he loved to recall words which Ruskin had spoken to him, that "the two most helpful bits of work a man can do for his time are to get people to observe carefully, and encourage them to describe accurately what they have seen." ' Hardwicke (Canon Rawnsley) never wearied in the task of awakening in children the desire to know, the power to think, and in developing ability to use hand and eyes; and this he regarded as a work in its very essence religious, for he believed that the love of truth and beauty lead men to God and Christ." Canon Rawnsley sought the friendship of teachers of all kinds, and "To the children of Crosthwaite schools the Vicar was almost as familiar a figure as one of their own masters. He would talk to the boys and girls on every kind of subject likely to interest them and awaken their intelligence. On the occasion of any function they were never forgotten, but were . . . allowed to take part in any event which would make a memory worth having in their lives. . . . He would carry them off on May day to the top of Crosthwaite tower to sing the Old Hundredth, would meet parties of them at the Keswick Museum and there lecture to them on the exhibits, would take to the school any visitor likely to interest them, and was never happier than in sharing their pleasures and in encouraging singing, dancing, carpentry and gymnastics. One of the first —if not the first—of the school gardens in the county was established at Crosthwaite, with its beehives and its barometer, and Hardwicke considered the effect of gardening on the boy mind to be almost magical :— ' New worlds of interest and of unexpected beauty open before him, he instinctively gives up doing damage to trees in blossom and growing shrubs. The boy watches a bird with different ideas, finds to his astonishment that it is better that the wise thrush should be left alone to bring off her brood, and seek and slay snails to feed them, than that he should take the first thrush's nest he can find.' " Canon Rawnsley gave prizes to children for competitive essays on birds and trees, formed the Cumberland Nature Club for their teachers, threw himself whole-heartedly " into the crusade which began with the introduction of a travelling dairy van, and ended with the establishment of that successful and useful institution, Newton Rigg County Farm School." Technical education, for mine and farm, owed much to him, and " As a pioneer of secondary education and the real founder of the Keswick High School, it was no wonder that his inspiring presence was demanded on the new Education Authority for Cumberland, and he very soon became chairman of the committee which dealt especially with secondary schools and higher education." He supplemented scholarships out of his own and his friends' pockets, and was the originator of the Secondary Schools Association in 1907.

Now we are all familiar with the fine work of the officials and teaching staff of schools—if we are not, we ought to be— but there is a world of difference between the routine of the professional educationist with Treasury or rate resources at his disposal, and that of the clergy. The latter are not primarily commissioned to teach in quite Rawnsley's way— and theirs is purely a work of supererogation. We have quoted him at some length : his individual work was not of overwhelming importance in itself. But when, as we claim to be true, this kind of work and sympathy and encouragement is multiplied all over the country so that Rawnsley's work is only typical of that of great numbers of rural and urban clergy, we do get a great mass of clerical achievement.

It lies outside the range of quantitative measurement and statistics, and is all the more vital for that very fact. The parson may often be an autocrat, but those of the old school were men who had inherited great privileges such as Rawnsley did from his home, and Uppingham under Thring, and Balliol under Jowett and they felt it a duty to pass on the legacy to their less fortunate fellow-citizens.

Another type of pioneer contributed to the evolution of the improved type of school curriculum that we know to-day. Some isolated examples may be given. An Oxford graduate, the Rev. John Smith, taught experimental science to a new generation of teachers-to-be at the Winchester Diocesan Training School.[53] The Froebel system much in vogue in the 20th century, is reported on by H.M. Inspector in 1855–6 at St. Mark's, Lavenham.[54] Then at the village school of Hitcham, Suffolk, we have an astounding spectacle. There the professor of botany at Cambridge, the Rev. J. S. Henslow (1798–1861), had settled and now taught along lines that would be " progressive " to-day.[55] All kinds of out-of-school activities—cricket matches and varied recreations, flower shows—were introduced. *The Dictionary of National Biography* speaks warmly : " In spite of farmers' opposition, he established schools, into which he introduced the voluntary study of botany with signal success, benefit clubs, cricket and athletic clubs, allotments, horticultural shows, and parish excursions. At the half-yearly flower shows he was in the habit of delivering most effective simple " lecturets," as he termed them, mainly on some of the specimens in his varied collection of economic products. On the occasion of the parish excursions, substituted by him for the orgies known as " tithe dinners," he accompanied his parishioners to Ipswich, Cambridge, Norwich, and to the London Exhibition of 1851." He was a member of the Senate of London University and an examiner : " Darwin, his favourite pupil, always expressed the highest regard for him." There is something impressive in the manner in which this really great man exercised his ministry so simply among East Anglian farm-folk. Two other places where elementary science was taught were Wellington and Rockwell Green.[56]

If our elementary education has progressed " by instalments," a large instalment indeed was provided by Lord Sandon's and further Acts to ensure compulsory attendance. The clergy here had already made their contribution. As early as

1845 that great eccentric, the benevolent and despotic Hawker of Morwenstow,[57] issued the following :

" Take Notice

The Vicar will attend St. Mark's schoolroom every Friday at three o'clock, to catechise the scholars, and at the Sunday school at the usual hour. He will not from henceforth show the same kindness to those who keep back their children from school as he will to those who send them. ' Thou shalt not seethe a kid in his mother's milk ' *(Exod. xxiii. 19)."*

But few men could carry this off, and others find " voluntary compulsion " possible only by less direct means. The Rev. M. W. Currie,[58] feeling that " the early employment of children was a serious evil," in Feb., 1871, called a meeting of rate-payers, who unanimously voted against setting up a school board. The rector promised to manage and maintain the school at his own expense for three years, " on condition that they would all agree to employ no child in the parish who shall not have previously satisfied Her Majesty's Inspector at the annual examination in reading, writing and arithmetic, under Standard IV (Article 48 of the *Revised Code,* 1870)." Some boys came back to school from the land, but all the farmers and parents (after the rector had made a stand) loyally kept to their bargain. School pence rose in 3 years from £11 to £16, and there was a high average attendance.

The rector of Thornhill had a similar scheme for " indirect compulsory education," [59] and much earlier the Rev. J. B. Owen,[60] in 1857, propounded *Indirect Compulsory Schooling: a Scheme submitted to the Educational Conference* which shows how clearly some clergy at least saw the need for a radical change in the general attitude to elementary schooling. In the previous year the Hon. and Rev. G. M. Yorke tells in his *School and Workshop* (1856) of attempts to secure better school attendance by securing priority of employment to holders of the Committee of Council's leaving Certificate of 1855.

I. THE NEW ERA: 1870–1941

INTO the fevered struggles centring round the 1870 Act we
are not, fortunately, required to enter and at this stage we
are regarding Mr. Forster's Bill as a thing accomplished. One
quotation, however, may conveniently be given here from
Moneypenny and Buckle's *Life of Disraeli* [1] as a summary:
" The general sense of the House and of the country was that
the Bible should be read and that there should be religious
education in all schools, guarded by a conscience clause; but
the Radicals and the bulk of the Dissenters pressed for an
entirely secular system. This the Government could not concede: but they ultimately accepted a compromise, proposed
by Cowper-Temple, a Whig, providing that, while the Bible
should be read and explained, no catechism or other distinctive
formulary should be taught in a board school. Disraeli
immediately fastened on the weakness of this arrangement.
The schoolmaster could not, he pointed out, teach, enforce,
and explain the Bible without drawing some conclusions, and
what could these be but dogmas? ' You will not entrust the
priest or the presbyter,' he said, ' with the privilege of ex-
pounding the Holy Scripture to the scholars; but for that
purpose you are inventing and establishing a new sacerdotal
class. The schoolmaster who will exercise their function will
exercise an extraordinary influence upon the history of
England and upon the conduct of Englishmen.' "

We may say that the National Society's line in the 1870–1
Report [2] was eminently fair and reasonable: a " live and let
live " spirit. It is claimed—and this claim must be judged
by the standards of 1870—that the church has adequately
provided for the nation's needs in education, and much
material is quoted from the 1866–7 survey by the society. It
is contended on p. 15 that on the average each child receives
four and a half years' schooling. This average figure includes
the " longer school life " children, and the lot of those whose
schooling was shorter than the average is recognized as being
very bad, even if the responsibility does rest with the parents. [3]

In the year covered by the report £12,528 had been given
by the society towards the erection of schools and teachers'
residences, and a capitation grant of £2 10s. was made for

every student who had resided for one year in the training colleges and passed the examinations of H.M. Inspectors. The church training colleges had been very badly hit by the Revised Code's reduction of grants.[4]   The society allocated £914 for books for schools and the receipts in the depository were £34,563, a rise of £2,219 over the previous year.

The Treasurer, Archdeacon Sinclair, begged to retire after thirty years' service.   " As Secretary, as Treasurer and always as adviser and benefactor he has contributed, perhaps more than any other member, to the success of the National Society." [5]   But the times are critical and demand renewed effort, for the society needs all its resources and the support of churchmen.   In the new order that we know to-day things may be forgotten and it is well to note the changes that led to the improved state of affairs now acclaimed.   " The Society began its work when the Church and nation were wholly apathetic about national education; when it was even hotly contested whether it were safe to promote the education of the poor.   In that day, there were no model schools, no systems of training, and no adequate school literature.   The office of schoolmaster was held in contempt.   Schoolrooms were few and badly built.   Schools were without inspection, without control, without encouragement and without success. The Society applied itself to create a better state of things." [6] As these words bring us to a retrospective view of what the church had accomplished under the voluntary system it may be well to reinforce them by some remarks of an acute and greatly respected schoolmaster and churchman, the late Ven. J. M. Wilson.[7]   " The history of Elementary Education in England, so far as I understand it, differs in very important respects from that in other countries; but I do not remember to have seen the difference pointed out.   In England the public conscience was not generally awake to the need of education in the earlier half of this century, and such schools as previously existed for the working classes were the creation of the S.P.C.K. and similar religious associations or individuals.   It is correct to say that elementary education in England was at first supplied entirely from the Christian enthusiasm and love and patriotism of religious bodies—of course, in particular, the Church of England.   The whole system of Day Schools and Colleges was thus erected, not by the Nation, but by the Churches, or by the general religious character of the education given.   The whole conception,

moreover, of training the teacher is English, and it is religious.
It was a training for a religious duty. The Churches under-
rate their work. The whole of the National System is the
creation of religious enterprise and liberality and forethought,
and is imbued with the spirit. It was a marvellous achievement. In face of inexperience and ignorance and much
opposition [8]—arising from a general distrust of education
among the working classes, shared by squires, farmers, manu-
facturers and labourers alike—the Churches did work out a
practical scheme for a National system of education on which
the greater system of to-day is built. The nation has adopted
it, but forgets its origin."

It is strongly urged that all educational needs should be
now met by churchmen in order to leave no room for state,
secular or undenominational schools. A " Special Appeal " [9]
on the lines of the old Queen's Letter was submitted to the
archbishops and bishops and raised £13,115 by the close of
the year. " But this opportunity once lost, will not recur "
and it is claimed that " The National Society is identified
with, and has been a promoter of, five-sixths of the schools
now available in England and Wales for the education of
the poor." The extent of the society's final effort to consolidate church schools was magnificent: 1,411 grants
totalling £63,600.[10] " The proposed expenditure on these
schools, calculated to accommodate 195,000 children, is
estimated at £848,000." [11] New applications for aid come in
daily and a deficit of £33,420 of sums promised must be
raised. The S.P.C.K. repeats its generous actions of the past
by sending £10,000 towards the cost of building and enlarging
schools.

Now that the 1870 Act forbade H.M.Is to inspect religious
education, paid diocesan inspectors are advocated ; more, they
were requested by a meeting of secretaries of diocesan boards.
The National Society promised to help, and the S.P.C.K.
gave £3,000.

The depository's receipts amounted to £35,896, being more
than tenfold the figures of 1848, the year of commencement.

In 1872 the committee reported that it had taken the un-
precedented step of suspending grants, but only because their
" entire income was pledged for two years in advance," to
the extent of £57,763.[11] To illustrate the extent to which
the publishing and distributing side of the National Society's
work was helping education we may notice that the de-

pository's turn-over was £39,437, and on p. 43 of the 1872
report of the National Society is a list of branch depositories,
with those of the S.P.C.K.

The operations of the Endowed Schools Commissioners, it
is regretted, leave much doubt as to the future of middle-class
schools and no progress is consequently made by the *ad hoc*
committee of the society.

It is surprising to see that there was an increase in subscriptions, donations and church collections,[12] for the natural
tendency of churchmen was to assume that the State was
relieving them of the moral obligation to care for the education of the poor. Indeed, grants were made for the extension
of the church training colleges, and some surprise is chronicled
that " male and female students " show a remarkable equality
in the division of honours at the common examination. A
grant of £100 is made to the Bishop Otter Memorial College
at Chichester, where " a few ladies " of a somewhat higher
social position are to be trained to accept positions as
teachers.[13] It may be hoped that this unctuousness in pre-
serving the proprieties of Victorian class distinctions did not
strike such a jarring note with contemporaries.

It may now be convenient to depart from the narrative of
events to meet a criticism of the church's work for the education of the people on the ground of motive. The view is
sometimes taken that the church's efforts to further the provision of elementary education was inspired by a zeal, however fine, that was coloured by merely " sectarian motives."
Now Her Majesty's Inspectors knew the field of education
as few men could pretend to do and their considered reports
are worthy of careful study. The religious conflict was carefully planned by interested parties outside the schools : inside
them, says the *Committee of Council Report* of 1870–1, we
have no proselytizing and no Nonconformist suspicions of it.
Nay, two British schools united with church schools and
" such Nonconformists have at the same time handed over
their subscriptions for the support of these united schools."
Two instances are given of endowed dissenting schools that
engaged church teachers, both communicants. " This tends
to show that in some places the religious difficulty is treated
as it ought to be, as a sentiment and not a fact." [14]   In the
largest school in one inspector's district there were only four
cases in 10–12 years of complaints about the religious difficulty.[15]   In another school in a period of 12 years there were

no complaints at all from the parents of 4,113 children.[16] After paying tribute to the educational zeal and generosity of the clergy, one of the inspectors said that he had never met the difficulty in any rural parish, where the chief danger, in "single school areas," was said to be! "And when the history of Voluntary schools comes to be written, and the facts connected with their establishment and support quietly and fairly considered, I think it will be established that the self-denial of the clergy in school-work and their interest in elementary education have not arisen from a desire to do the impossible work of making converts in a party sense of little children, but rather from the more Catholic and sensible desire, the earnest wish to see their parishioners more intelligent, more cultivated, more refined—in a word, more educated." [17]   A further quotation may serve to stress the point. " I forget who the famous Scandinavian historian was who wrote his remarkable chapter XXXIX on ' Snakes in Iceland ' thus briefly, There are no snakes in Iceland, but I feel his difficulty in commenting on the religious difficulty. There is none; it has evaporated. . . . In Church of England schools the time-table and section 7 of the Education Act have been most cordially accepted, most honourably observed. The Nonconformists have acted with similar readiness, nor can I find any violation of conscience anywhere." [18]   Later, another H.M.I. thought that he had found his Icelandic snake in the person of a boy withdrawn from a class, especially since this took place in a school belonging to the Cowley Fathers! The facts, however, are rather disappointing. The boy's mother was an ardent Good Templar who objected to a poetry lesson dealing with John Gilpin of Cowper's poem as a man who " loved liquor."

To return to the story of the National Society: in 1873 the voluntary income of £17,333 was, save in the previous year, the highest ever received since the Queen's Letter ceased and was claimed as the best evidence of the confidence the Society enjoyed.[19]   The Society's Depository had a turn-over of £42,417. The Middle-class schools make but little progress, although it is recorded that many elementary schools are saved from being handed over to the state. A list, con-tinued in later reports, appears in 1874,[20] and shows the district secretaries and treasurers. It makes clear, again, the extent to which the Society depended on local effort.

In the 1875 report [21] we see that the National Society had voted £91,043 since the 1870 Act to help schools. This was part of a total expenditure of £1,456,466 and accommodation was provided for 293,999 children.[22] But the competition of Board schools when they undercut church schools is severe,[23] and subscriptions to local schools are falling off in sums varying from £1 to £60. Yet the total voluntary offerings continue to rise and beat all records: £19,135.[24] Churchmen were obviously prepared to make sacrifices to ensure the popular provision of church teaching. Diocesan inspection is now universal and examinations in religious knowledge show the women's colleges ahead of the men's! As time goes on, however, there is noted a "disproportionate increase" in the number of Board Schools.[25] The figures do suggest that the voluntary system was of itself unable to meet the entire needs of the people, but it is well to remember that the Board schools made most progress in the large urban areas where the parochial system was often very weak.

A sign of the times was the end of the old *Monthly Paper*. It was superseded by *The School Guardian,* a weekly periodical more fitted to contemporary standards.

It is claimed that in the year ended Aug. 31st, 1876[26] churchpeople gave £592,300 (as against £528,483 in the previous year), towards the cost of church schools. Additional accommodation was provided for 96,223 children, despite some transfers of church schools to school Boards. The Society had a real task in seeing that school managers stood by the moral obligation of their trust deeds, and a new "Union Clause" was to be introduced into all further trust deeds[27] to prevent recently helped schools from transference without the National Society's consent.

The sum of £5,948 is granted to schools and small amounts paid to certificated teachers to enable their respective schools to qualify for the Government grant. But there continued to be a rapid increase in the number of scholars in Board schools—in church schools it was 65,790—for compulsory attendance came in with Lord Sandon's Act of 1876. The following figures to show the volume of effort under the voluntary system are at least interesting.[28]

Voluntary Subscriptions towards Annual Maintenance.

Church Schools	in 1876	£592,300,	*in 1877*	£620,034	
Nonconformist Schools	,,	,,	£105,380,	,, ,,	£104,930
Roman Catholic	,,	,,	£50,638,	,, ,,	£57,459

The society stresses the importance of having duly qualified
and properly equipped teachers and sets aside £8,000 to
augment a still larger sum put up by the S.P.C.K. towards
the cost of building a new training college for women at
Tottenham,[29] and £10,000 for new accommodation at
Battersea. Then poor schools need help: the Poor School
Relief Fund for the metropolis had collected large sums
through the instrumentality of the committee of the National
Society, who elsewhere set aside £5,000 to be voted to local
boards who could themselves raise a minimum of £250.[30]

In the years 1879–1880 progress was made along the
traditional lines by the National Society, but the growth of
Board schools did come to force the surrender of some
church schools,[31] although many were saved by the society's
intervention. It is comforting to see that the Birmingham
School Board saw by experience the folly of dispensing with
moral instruction and soon resumed it.

The 1881 report of the National Society covered a decade
of the new era and will be examined in some detail.[32] The
statistics taken from the Education Department returns of
May, 1881 show the remarkable mass achievement of the
voluntary system in day schools. Since 1870 the elementary
school population has doubled itself, as the Government
returns show. The School Boards " with their practically un-
limited resources have created accommodation for 1,082,634
children: Christian zeal and energy, unaided by the rates,
have in exactly the same period, provided accommodation
for 1,279,535." [33] The church is still educating twice as many
children as the Board Schools, nor were the latter without
reproach. " The School Board at Hartlebury is in default,
having done nothing to build a school for that populous
parish, except to purchase a site which cannot be conveyed.
What the school board, however, is bent on not doing the
new rector and his friends will do, and a school for 220 is
at once to be built." [34] An inspector had earlier to refer " to
the considerable number of school boards which had no
schools under their control, and this affords an explanation
of the comparatively high percentage (15·8% of current
income) of the charges for administration and miscellaneous
expenses." [35] A satisfactory school depended on good management, and here church schools were probably pre-eminent,
with Board schools the least satisfactory in this respect. " In
a rural parish, the objections to a school board, summarily

stated, are the dislike entertained by the great body of the clergy of the Established Church, and the expense. The former I do not find so prominent as at first : in many cases the clergyman has accepted his true position, which in a Church parish is that of Chairman of the school board, and finds that he has about as much power as in a voluntary public elementary school, his colleagues probably taking little interest in education : so that he is supporting the school at other people's expense instead of his own, as was most likely the case before the board was formed." This was the view of an H.M.I. speaking of the west Somerset district.[36]

The growth in the cost per pupil of elementary education, owing to higher standards of equipment required by the Education Department, rapidly increased. " Managers, too, have been steadily learning the lesson that there is no source of income so sure and so important as that which is furnished by the scholars themselves. Instead of charging a penny a week, which was the prevailing fee a few years ago, many of them now require 3d., 4d., or even 6d., and they find, in the great majority of cases, that parents are neither unable nor unwilling to pay the increased fee." [37]   Managers should be active in every branch of school life and parents should pay all they can afford. Religious education must not be neglected, paid inspectors of schools are necessary, and diocesan funds for helping poor schools should be set up. The dangers of church school transference are stressed, and the committee of the National Society wisely attacks the 4th Schedule of the Education *Code* on the ground that to teach Latin, French, Botany, etc, in an elementary school (of 1881) was wasteful. The following qualification is noteworthy. " They are alive to the importance of giving facilities for the study of any or all of them to the children of the labouring classes who show special aptitude. But such facilities . . . would be more efficiently provided through the foundation of scholarships in secondary schools." [38]   It is claimed on the next page that there is an anomaly working against church schools, when the children of poor parents may go free to the Board schools, but must apply to the Board of Guardians direct for the fees at church schools.

In 1880 the " voluntary income " of the National Society was £16,118 out of a total of £21,312. A sum of £365 was voted to a fine effort in Liverpool, where a school costing £10,000 was being built for 1,100 children.[39] The report for 1882 [40] points out that the rating of voluntary schools, which already save the ratepayers' pockets vast sums, thereby compels them " to provide facilities for their own extinction." [41] This was indeed an anomaly of a cruel kind. Then board schools lack the personal contact of those interested in them, and an H.M.I.'s report is quoted as saying that they " often appear to deteriorate in their general tone and behaviour." [42]

In the 1883 annual report [43] the figures are given of expenditure by churchpeople on schools and training colleges from Government returns and National Society records. The vastness of these figures by contemporary standards is very difficult for us to realize to-day. The year's expenditure on school maintenance was £581,179 as compared with £582,382 in the previous year. On p. 11 of the report are recited some assurances with regard to the 1870 Act by Mr. Forster and Mr. Gladstone (but not embodied in the text), the main point of which was that the Board schools were not to compete with or displace voluntary schools, but to supplement them. A memorial from the National Society has been sent to the G.O.M. [44] The Depository sold £51,162 worth of goods : in the year 1884, perhaps mainly owing to the requirements of the new code, the figures were £57,810. [45]

The *Report* for the year 1886 [46] is chiefly concerned with what it terms " over pressure in schools " occasioned by Lowe's " payment by results " system, " vexatious requirements unknown in other countries."

In 1887 for the first time there is a decrease in the number of children in church schools—5,532—a temporary relapse only. This leads us to study a new set of decennial figures, in the 1891 *Report*. [47] A few schools were surrendered by the church and went to swell the figures of the Board Schools, yet there was a net increase of 2,528 scholars in the last year. The number of added school places was 29,978.

An unusual feature of the 1893 *Report* [48] is that the late Mr. R. Berridge left £40,000 for the promotion of instruction in cookery in church elementary schools, and the fact that it was left to the National Society is a tribute to its educational as well as religious character. This benefaction was of great practical value in later years, and the work continues at Hampstead. [49] The Berridge Fund is now administered under a scheme of the Board of Education dated Dec. 21st, 1904.

The struggle between the Voluntary and the Board schools

is commented on with great fairness by the Archbishops'
Report, quoted in full in the National Society's *Report* of
1895.[50] We are not concerned with its controversial aspects,
but we may note the remarks of the Truro Diocesan Inspector
a little later to illustrate the stand the church was making for
the cause of religious education.[51]

We have not hitherto noticed a new kind of local association—the " Associations of Voluntary Schools." [52] Schools
pooled their financial balances and generally acted in a co-
operative manner for their mutual and common benefit. An
instance may be cited : " From the office of the Sheffield
Church Elementary Day School Aid Association I have been
favoured with the following information (Feb., 1895):—
Our Schools' Emergency Fund has collected £4,500, which
has been apportioned amongst the more needy of the Sheffield
Church Day Schools to enable them to comply with the
requirements of Circular 321. *In every* (italics quoted) case,
the parish aided is required to meet the grant made by a
local (italics quoted) contribution, such local contributions
amounting in the aggregate to another £4,500. Of this
further sum about £2,000 has already been raised. Some
schools have been improved without any help from the central
fund, but the amount spent cannot yet be ascertained." [53]

And some co-operated for the sake of the principle of
religious education under the Voluntary System alone : " He
notes much money spent in Salisbury and Winchester on
repairs, additions, and improvements, and in the latter city
a curious co-operation of all the voluntary schools, consisting
of ten Church of England, one Roman Catholic, and one
Wesleyan, all willingly rating themselves to a common fund
for these purposes." [54]

It is clearly shown in the National Society's 1898 report [55]
that the percentage of attendances in voluntary schools is
higher than that of Board schools, and notice is made of a
legacy of £11,820 received the previous year. A résumé of
draft bills of various kinds and reports of several church
committees over the period 1894–1901 is given in the 1901
Report, but they are mainly of technical interest. Statistics
may be quoted again, leaving aside figures for accommodation and numbers on the register.[56]

There was thus a slight fall in the number of average
attendances in church schools, but a rise in the number of
special places provided. The Board of Education (which had

replaced the Education Department in August 1899) could only furnish returns of voluntary contributions for the support of non-provided schools which are from the nature of the case very imperfect. But the National Society's *Report* of 1901 (p. 29) shows that " when everything is taken into account, it is below rather than above the mark to say that Churchmen spend on their schools and colleges annually *one million of their own money* (italics quoted)." With the figures before us [57] to represent the immense volume of mass achievement by the Church of England in the field of popular education we may leave the first part of the New Era of State Education —1870–1902.

The Act of 1902 abolished the school boards and placed education on a municipal basis. It was claimed by some that the church benefited by the passing of the Act. But " So far from the Church deriving any pecuniary benefit from the Act, it contributes towards the secular education of the people a very large annual sum, very much more than the cost of distinctive Church teaching, which the Nonconformists declare to be in part paid by themselves. Your Committee hold that the settlement which the Act has made with Church Schools is as follows. The Church will give value to the Government of about £715,000 a year. This is a very low estimate of the annual value of her buildings at $3\frac{1}{4}\%$. The buildings in open market would probably fetch a good deal more, therefore it is quite fair to say that the Church is *giving* (italics quoted) the State an annual value of at least £715,000. Now, the total cost of the maintenance of Church Schools throughout England and Wales is £4,399,267. Out of this, £175,970 represents the fraction proportionate to the time spent in teaching *distinctive Church formularies* (italics quoted) which are not allowed by the Cowper-Temple clause. This £175,970 is a liberal estimate of the money spent upon teaching which the conscience of the Nonconformists *objects* (italics quoted) to pay for. So that the Church is contributing to the Elementary Education of the country by giving the use of her buildings rent free, an equivalent to £715,000. Therefore a balance of £539,030 is the Church's contribution towards the cost of the public secular education. And let it be further remembered that in addition to paying the rent Churchmen are going to do all the landlord's repairs." [58] Despite the note of petulance (and even of unconscious humour in the final paragraph), these words bear sincere

witness to the church's vital contribution of resources that
were the very basis of all subsequent State education.

The work for national education of Archbishop Frederick
Temple is recalled by the institution of a special fund for
assisting church schools and bearing his name: £9,360 was
contributed to it in 1904.[59]

The period 1904–1914 is not of great interest as far as the
history of the National Society is concerned: the controversy over the 1906 education bill is well commented on in
Bell's *Randall Davidson*. A domestic event was the move to
the present home in Gt. Peter Street in 1905. The Society
was now in the position of a purely voluntary society with
no official standing in the world of state education, however
much it represented the church's official views on the
elementary education question.

A Departmental Committee on Educational Endowments
was set up in 1910 and the Archbishop of Canterbury was
invited to nominate two persons to give evidence on behalf of
the Church of England—one of these was Mr. R. Holland, at
that time Assistant Secretary of the National Society. The
Departmental Committee issued its report in 1911.

Below is a list of grants made to schools,[60] showing that
the society continued to play its historic part.[61] We may
record that in the last year before the Great War of 1914–18
voluntary subscriptions to the National Society were greater
than in any year since 1874, namely £21,634, an unimpeach-
able tribute to the confidence reposed in the society by
English churchmen and their continued faith in the principles
of religious education. That the race of princely benefactors
to the cause of church elementary education had not ceased
is shown by Mr. T. F. Harrison's gift of £15,000 for
St. Anne's School, Stanley, Liverpool, to accommodate 900
children.[62] We see that the number of pupils of all kinds at
the National Society's Training College for Teachers of
Domestic Subjects at Berridge House, West Hampstead was
a record—281.[63] Another " outlier," the hostel for women
students—the society had always adopted as a cardinal
principle the necessity of residential training colleges—at
Goldsmith's College training to be teachers began to meet
competition from that of the education authorities,[64] but it
survived until 1939.

Indeed, from 1904, when Mr. A. T. Lawrence, K.C. issued
his report after a public inquiry into the default of the Car-

marthenshire County Council to administer fairly the education acts by discriminating against church schools, to the notorious Swansea case of 1911 there was much strife in the world of education. Judgment was given for the National Society in the House of Lords on April 11th, 1911; without calling upon counsel for the Society the appeal of the Board of Education was dismissed. Every judge had previously taken the view of their lordships that the Board of Education had a statutory commission to see that the church schools were fairly treated. The case, with others, was a signal blow to the Board's reputation for integrity of administration, and was a disgraceful example of the evil practice of mingling party politics with education. These words will sound strange to all who know the friendliness and impartiality of the Board to-day.

" Within the last few years, as recent reports have shown, a quite new function of great importance has devolved upon the Society—viz., that of championing in the Law Courts the case of denominational schools which have suffered from the unjust administration at the hands of the local authorities or of the Board of Education." [65]

As the chairman of the London County Council Education Committee explicitly stated, the existence of voluntary schools saved the ratepayers several millions of taxation—he believed a capital expenditure of $4\frac{1}{2}$ millions: " the least of the blessings secured to London by its non-provided schools." [66]

Finally, we may note post-Great War developments.[67] The church's organization underwent changes and amplification, as shown, for example, in the case of the setting up of the Church Assembly and the Parochial Church Councils. In 1934 a supplemental charter was granted, relating the National Society—now known as " The National Society for promoting Religious Education in accordance with the Principles of the Church of England "—more closely to the Church Assembly, so that it becomes " The Central Council of the Church for Religious Education," and is charged with the wide mission of encouraging religious education in every way.

The century-old work for elementary education was and is being steadily carried forward, based, of course, on the traditional policy of helping local effort. The work for the training of teachers is noticed elsewhere.[68] In addition, the society is now charged with responsibility in regard to universities and university colleges; public, secondary and preparatory schools; voluntary education for children, youths and adults, such as Sunday schools, youth organizations and Church Tutorial Classes.[69]   These latter are the church's equivalent of the Workers' Educational Association, with Dr. Albert Mansbridge, C.H., as founder.

Of late years and especially since the granting of its 1934 Charter, the National Society has been much concerned in bringing the religious education in provided schools within the scope of its operations.   The Cowper-Temple clause states that " no religious catechism or formulary which is distinctive of any religious denomination " may be taught in a provided school, and the teachers in these schools are appointed by the local authorities without reference to their religious beliefs or their qualifications to give the religious instruction required by the school syllabus.   Many of the teachers in those schools have, however, been trained in the church training colleges and the religious teaching given by them is good both in spirit and in technique.   The National Society's Organizers for Religious Teaching have held training weeks or short training courses and have also assisted at training weeks organized by local authorities which have been largely attended by teachers in provided schools.

An important document illustrating co-operation between the Church of England and other bodies is given in full in Appendix IV.

To this may be added a further illustration of the spirit of the National Society, taken from Bell's *Life of Randall Davidson,* which will be readily appreciated by all who do not confuse adherence to principle with obscurantism.

" There was no religious controversy; and when the Act took its place on the Statute book in August [1918] the following letter reached him [Abp. Davidson] from its author :

Rt. Hon. H. A. L. Fisher to the Abp. of Canterbury.

Board of Education, Whitehall, London, S.W.

8/8/18.

" Now that the Education Bill has been placed on the Statute Book, you will allow me to tender you my most sincere and heartfelt thanks for the invaluable help which you have given me at every stage of the Bill, and more especially during its passage through the House of Lords.

" I feel also that I should like to tell you how very much I appreciate the wise and broad-minded attitude which Mr. Holland of the National Society has adopted throughout.

" He has kept us in touch with the body of opinion he represents, but has always stood for moderate and sensible Counsels, and I feel that we have been indeed fortunate in finding in the Secretary of the National Society a man of so balanced and generous a temper." [70]

It is interesting to note that the society wishes to help other churches with religious education, just as it has drawn on the services of Free Churchmen (like Dr. Basil Yeaxlee) for lectures and conferences,[71] and it is no breach of confidence on either side to say that the Society's relations with the Board of Education are uniformly friendly.

The Education Act of 1936 gave the Church a real opportunity in regard to the provision of senior schools. The Act allowed a Government grant up to 75% of the cost to the promoters of such schools and the National Society raised a fund, partly by special appeal and partly by allocation from its funds from annual revenue to assist in the provision of 75 senior schools, with a grant of 10% for the remaining cost. Large sums were also raised locally.

The Society publishes *The Bulletin* (3 times a year, later called the *News Sheet), The Teaching Church Review* (3 times a year), *The Church Teacher* (monthly) and works designed to fill special needs in elementary, secondary and Sunday schools. The Book Shop sales for the year ending March 31st, 1939, amounted to £24,000.

In recent years there has been a broadening of the conception of the true nature of education. The supposed distinction between secular and religious has disappeared. Old suspicions and mistrusts, as between denominations have diminished, and political animosities have largely died down. There is a far-reaching recognition of the need for co-operation in the work of religious education. An instance of inter-denominational co-operation is afforded by the Institute of Christian Education, which was brought into being in 1931, largely owing to the efforts of Canon Tissington Tatlow. Its work is to give expert advice to all engaged in the work of religious education at home and abroad. The institute publishes *Religion in Education* quarterly and maintains a reference library for the benefit of teachers.

Towards the end of 1940 the National Society's Standing

Committee appointed its Vice-Chairman, Canon Woodard (grandson of the founder of the Woodard Schools) as its special envoy to the dioceses to assist in the maintenance and setting up in every diocese of a comprehensive scheme of education in line with the fuller scope of the Society's 1934 Charter, and to ensure liaison between the society and the dioceses. The following paper has been issued for circulation in those dioceses that Canon Woodard is invited to visit for this purpose :—

THE CHURCH IN EDUCATION—1941

The National Society, as the Central Council of the Church for Religious Education, is submitting to the Dioceses of England and Wales a policy and plan for the furtherance of Religious Education.

Prolonged consultations with persons representing many and various interests in Education have led to the formulation of principles upon which we may hope to advance. The Archbishops of Canterbury, York and Wales have issued a statement and appeal entitled " Christian Education." The following quotation from this document provides both the starting point and the opportunity for the policy we now advocate :—" We regard our own Church Schools as a trust which should be preserved for the sake of the ideals for which they stand. Even if it may be admitted that in practice they sometimes fall short of these ideals, we earnestly appeal to all Church people to do their utmost to maintain them in real efficiency, and to see that they hold a place in the national system of education worthy of their high aims."

We retain this responsibility : and go on to advocate amongst other possible reforms in a wider field :—

A. ELEMENTARY SCHOOLS

i. That Religious Instruction should, equally with other subjects, be inspected by H.M. Inspectors or persons specially appointed for the purpose.

ii. That Religious Knowledge be included among the optional subjects which count for the Teachers' Certificate.

iii. That Local Education Authorities be urged to ensure that in all schools there are sufficient teachers willing and qualified to give Religious Instruction in accordance with the syllabus in use under the Authorities concerned, and in order to maintain a supply of such teachers Local Education Authorities be urged to increase the number of their courses in this subject and to facilitate and encourage attendance by their staffs at these or similar courses.

iv. That Section 10 of the Code of Regulations for Public Elementary Schools be amended so as to permit amongst the items enumerated upon the Time Table a short period for an opening service and that H.M. Inspector be instructed accordingly.

B. SECONDARY SCHOOLS

That in order to establish the principle that Divinity should be taught in the Secondary Schools of the Country and made continuous throughout the pupils' school life, the Board of Education be asked to use its influence with Local Authorities in regard to the following :—

(a) That the practice whereby Divinity takes its place with the other subjects and activities of the curriculum as a subject of inspection in Secondary Schools should be extended as widely as possible.

(b) That as far as possible there should be Divinity specialists on the staffs of Secondary Schools, as generally indicated in the Spens Report on Secondary Education.

(c) That encouragement should be given to teachers in Secondary Schools to qualify for the post of Divinity specialist by giving them leave of absence for the purpose of attending courses, by grants towards the fees for such courses, and towards travelling expenses.

C. UNIVERSITIES

The following resolution by the Standing Committee of the National Society, action in regard to which would involve an approach to the Universities, was agreed to and the Committee hoped that steps would be taken to approach the University Authorities in regard to it :—

" That it is desirable that in all Universities a degree course in Divinity should be available and that wherever practicable Divinity should be a subject qualifying for a general Honours or ordinary Degree."

The adoption of such reforms does not exhaust the possibility of further progress in the service of the Church to Education.

The National Society has entrusted to Canon Woodard the interpretation of this policy in the Dioceses, as and when he may be invited by diocesan Bishops for consultation.

There can be no hard and fast mode of procedure, but in response to many requests the following programme is suggested :

1. Diocesan Bishops may wish to consult their Councils or Boards of Education and other executive officers in the Diocese before seeking wider support for the policy outlined above.

2. After such consultation a review of diocesan organization in Religious Education, having regard to conditions at present and in the immediate future, will show whether financial resources and man-power are being used to the best advantage.

3. It is hoped also that as a result of this review closer co-operation will be established between diocesan organizations and the National Society—the Central Council of the Church for Religious Education.

4. The Bishop will consider the advisability of making known the situation with regard to Religious Education through his Diocesan Conference or otherwise.

5. There may follow a system of inquiry by a central group led by the Bishop, or his representative, and dividing into local groups of Clergy, Ministers, Administrators and Teachers. Such a group would assess the adequacy of Religious Education as at present administered in the Diocese, and make any necessary recommendations for improvement.

6. It should then be opportune to obtain evidence of large and varied support for the policy proposed above.

NATIONAL SOCIETY'S OFFICE,

March, 1941.

J. THE WORK OF OTHER CENTRAL BODIES

The history of the National Society has furnished the back-bone of the study of the church's contribution to elementary education since 1833, but, as may be frequently noticed, there were other agencies at work. The chief of these was the British and Foreign School Society, founded in 1814 on an undenominational basis. Of the origin of the Society, Dean Gregory wrote in his handbook *Elementary Education* as follows:—

"Dr. Andrew Bell and Mr. Joseph Lancaster were respectively the champions of rival sets of schools, and much useless and acrimonious controversy was raised as to their respective claims to priority of invention. Their plan was to employ monitors to a great extent, so that under the guidance of one head teacher a large number of children might receive instruction. The discussion of their proposals infused new life and vigour into the efforts for promoting education, by attracting attention to the subject. Mr. Lancaster was first in the field in England, whilst Dr. Bell had previously introduced his plan at Madras. At first, the Archbishop of Canterbury and several other Church dignitaries favoured Mr. Lancaster's plan; but when they found that the Church Catechism was not allowed to be taught in his schools, and that the religious teaching was avowedly of an un-denominational character, they withdrew; and they re-solved, under the auspices of Dr. Bell, to establish Church Schools to be taught on the monitorial or mutual instruc-tion system. Sounder views respecting modes of teaching have long since superseded the plan then adopted, but the impetus it gave to education has been lasting, and has produced abundant fruit. To originate and sustain schools founded on Dr. Bell's system, it was thought desirable by the Archbishop of Canterbury and the lead-ing members of the Society for Promoting Christian Knowledge that the Church should have a separate society, whose exclusive object should be the promotion of elementary education in England and Wales. In consequence, the National Society for Promoting the Education of the Poor in the Principles of the Established Church was founded on October 16th, 1811, and in 1817 it was incorporated by Royal Charter. The sup-porters of Mr. Lancaster's schools formed themselves into

a committee for developing schools upon his (undenominational) system, which eventually in 1814 assumed
the title of the British and Foreign Schools Society."

It will be right to regard the considerable achievement of
this society as being, in part, the work of Churchmen since its
original supporters were drawn from all denominations. It is
in the educational ideals rather than in the composition of the
membership that the difference between the British and
Foreign School Society and the National Society is to be
found. Undenominationalism attempts to divorce religious
teaching from ecclesiastical or institutional practice. The
National Society, on the other hand, has always stood for that
presentation of the Christian Faith which finds its balanced
expression in the Book of Common Prayer.

The Home and Colonial Infant School Society[1] was
founded in 1836, and in 1845 became the Home and Colonial
Infant and Juvenile School Society, since it was not merely
concerned with infant education. The Rev. Charles Mayo first
introduced the methods of Pestalozzi to England, and with his
sister Elizabeth was the real driving force in the Society.

Here is an early account : " The Society was founded in
February, 1836, having for its proposed objects the improvement of the system of infant education, the education of
teachers, and the creation of one or more model schools.
The first report, made in Feb. 1837, states with much force
the reasons that suggested the formation of the society. ' The
Committee may without fear of contradiction assert that
few situations in life require so much discretion, so much
energy, so much tenderness, so much self-control, and love,
as that of a teacher of babes : that to guide and govern an
infant school calls for wisdom to discern, versatility to modify,
firmness to persevere, judgment to decide ; and they may
add that no uneducated or undisciplined mind can supply
the incessant care, the watchful diligence, the unwearied
patience necessary to manage young children.' "[2]

The Gray's Inn Road Institution opened in 1836 and 48
of the 120 candidates were rejected because they lacked the
necessary qualifications. The first tasks included the founding
of a model school, a juvenile school, and the preparation of
text-books. The model school accommodated 60 persons and
cost £1,500. In the years 1836-46 as many as 1443 teachers
were trained, who paid £7,725 out of a total cost of £22,687,
leaving the Society a sum of roughly £1,500 a year to find.
The religious position of the Society was quite clear. It

was a church society " for Training Teachers and for the Improvement and Extension of Education on Christian Principles as such Principles are set forth and embodied in the Doctrinal Articles of the Church of England." Churchmen and dissenters learnt their lessons in class together, but —strange tribute to the real influence of personal contacts between students living together—they boarded separately! Of the 50 pupils, 33 were churchpeople; married men (but not bachelors) and women were admitted.[3] But the Society's financial position suggests that the volume of support from churchpeople was hardly adequate.[4]

A brief historical note of the society is contained in its report for 1902–3.[5] At the end of its second year 172 students had been sent out, and the figure to date is given : " 7,000 trained teachers, each bearing, more or less distinctly, the impress of their surroundings there : and each becoming, it is hoped, a centre for the diffusion of the highest truth, in the sphere where God has placed them." This year saw the move from Gray's Inn Road to Wood Green, and funds for the new college collected to date amounted to £11,850.[6] By the time of the 1906–7 report a venture at Highbury was styled the " Highbury Hill Training College," and it had a " High School " attached for the preliminary training of intending teachers, of whom 23 lived in the college. But in 1909 the report [7] tells of its transference to a new board of management composed of a majority of L.C.C. representatives and the place lost its church character. The society now concentrated all its efforts on Wood Green, and in 1924–5 the report shows subscriptions of £54 and donations of £111, hardly a satisfactory position.

When Wood Green came under the Board of Supervision for Church Training Colleges the society had served its purpose and represented hardly anybody's views. But the closing of Wood Green College in 1928 was regretted. The site was sold in 1929, the 200 places in the college were distributed amongst the other church colleges, and after discharge of all liabilities, the proceeds of sale were allocated, with the Board of Education's approval, to the extension and improvement of St. Mary's College, Cheltenham, and the society itself ceased to exist. But it had served its generations well, had outgrown its usefulness and finally fell a victim to the call for rationalization and large scale organization of the training colleges.

Other societies directly concerned with education in some way or other that are still flourishing may be mentioned. The

Church Schoolmasters' and Schoolmistresses' Benevolent Institution was founded in 1857 and still does good work.[8] The Church Teachers' Fellowship[9] and the Church Managers' and Teachers' Association[10] are still able also to co-ordinate the work of their members. The Church Extension Association[11] aids religious training and the education of children in schools and orphanages. It conducts missions for very poor children and gives them holidays in the country and by the sea. The dividing line between the provision of popular education by churchmen at their own expense and what we might more usually call philanthropic and charitable work proper is not clear and at best would be arbitrary. There was a vast amount of effort and achievement which had for its object the improvement of the lot of the poor which included in its scope much educational work, although this was not of primary importance. Within the scale of the present essay only the more important aspects of this philanthropic effort can be afforded the barest reference.

The Society for Bettering the Condition of the Poor had been founded in 1795 by Bishop Barrington of Durham, and in its title it reflects the wishes and intentions of great numbers of churchmen. It embodied the XVIIIth century tradition of charitable enterprise that was most noticeably continued in the work of Shaftesbury and others for the ragged children, and Preb. Rudolf for the " Waifs and Strays." This work was generally carried on as a joint effort by men of good will of all shades of belief, but the mainspring was the Christian conscience, as in the case of the Ragged School Union.[12]

Complementary to this deep-rooted evangelical tradition was the work of the Christian Socialists and here we may mention Maurice, Kingsley, Hughes and Ludlow. A convenient study of their contribution to English life and thought will be found in the works of the Rev. G. C. Binyon and D. O. Wagner.[13] In our own times their spirit has lived on in men like Canon Scott Holland, Bishop Charles Gore—the extent of whose influence was enormous—and the Church Union Summer School of Sociology,[14] the Industrial Christian Fellowship, and other agencies. As we look at these to-day we notice a fusion of the tractarian's special contribution with those qualities that Maurice and his friends had so vividly represented, and this combination of politico-economic realism with a real insistence on theological principle has naturally included genuine contributions to the theory of education, and the problem of leisure and allied subjects.[15]

An educational and social phenomenon of great importance in its day was the Settlement movement and this is still very active. It was primarily educational, but its results were much more widely beneficial. " The father of all Settlements was Toynbee Hall. But Toynbee Hall would never have existed if in 1873 Samuel Barnett, who had just married Henrietta Rowland, had not declined the offer of a country living, and become Vicar of St. Jude's, Whitechapel." [16] The university and public school missions have played their part nobly in affording their members the opportunity of sympathetic service to those less well situated than themselves.

Much educational work is done in obscurity by the various religious communities, with rescue and preventive work— some of this is listed in the annual *Church of England Year Book,* with allied activities.[17] There are five residential institutions, run by the church, for the Blind, and as early as 1838 an exclusively anglican society, the London Society for Teaching the Blind to Read, was founded. There is a Church Central Advisory Council to co-ordinate work with the deaf and dumb population, and the S.P.C.K. gives much help.

Finally, we must mention Queen's College for Women, founded in 1848, which arose out of the Governesses' Benevolent Institution, and the Working Men's College,[18] Gt. Ormond St., that sprang into existence in 1854. Both these still go on and they owe an incalculable debt to the life and labours of Frederick Denison Maurice. The Rev. Freeman Wills was Secretary of the Recreative Evening Schools Association and in his *Church Polytechnics for Younger Men and Lads* (1888) he tells us that the Finsbury Polytechnic, opened the previous year, had 6,000 lads on the books and 1,000 on the waiting list.

No attempt in this chapter can be made to indicate more than a few only of the types of charitable enterprise related to popular education, for which the church is directly or indirectly responsible. But it is well to remember that these are often pioneer efforts in social amelioration as her schools were in education, and where the church led the way the state followed. In some directions the work is specifically religious and the state has not encroached, or is cognizant of its unfitness for the task. Much of the work is essentially local or private and no record exists of a vast amount of charitable work by clergy and laity whose deeds are known only in a tiny circle of the Household of Faith.

K. THE CHURCH'S TRAINING COLLEGES

THE Committee of Council issued minutes for a National Normal School on April 13th, 1839,[1] but these were cancelled on June 3rd, since religious thought condemned the state's intrusion into what was regarded as a spiritual sphere. James Phillips Kay (later Sir James Kay-Shuttleworth)[2] then founded a private Training School at Battersea, which he has himself described.[3] This institution comes into our story when it was taken over by the National Society and it happens that the 1845 report[4] of the Committee of Council describes it in very great detail, just after it had been taken over. Great progress was made under the Rev. T. Jackson. Under the former management the majority of the students came from pauper unions!

In Sept. 1844 there were 24 students when transferred.

In Oct. 1845 there were 67 students, and at the time of the report this was increased to 72.

The original founders had a special reason for going to Battersea : " In the selection of the locality, they were influenced by a desire to avail themselves of the co-operation of the Hon. and Rev. Robt. Eden, the vicar of Battersea, to whose great experience in matters connected with elementary education and his judgment, not less than to the countenance and zealous support which he has extended to it, the Institution owes the greatest obligations."

Mention has been made[5] of some of the early work by the National Society and the local diocesan boards.[6] What were the ideals of these training colleges? We must begin our answer by saying that there was a temptation for the smaller diocesan colleges to acquiesce in the desire of their pupils, who had the very slenderest of means, to cut down their course of training to something far below what *we* might think adequate. In fact, what was done was about all that was practicable in the economic circumstances. From that day to this the training of school teachers has been subsidized. But the ideals that were always present, say, in St. Mark's, Chelsea were of the highest order, and soon spread throughout the system. The College was to be a family of young men who have answered a vocation, who live a common life of work, worship and recreation, specially designed to enrich and develop the individual personality. The common life was the keynote of the system, and the training for a consecrated life of service was considered of greater importance (" character ") than the acquisition of mere technical efficiency (" instruction ") and the church (despite the exception of the college at Norwich) has always regarded " day training colleges " as inadequate.

In the *Memorials of St. Mark's College* we read :

" It had been the original idea of the founders of this College that the schoolmaster should be trained for the Diaconate, and should carry on the work of the National Schoolmaster in that capacity. This was the origin of the name St. Mark's. ' Take Mark and bring him with thee, for he is profitable to me for the Ministry.' As a matter of fact many of the old students were ordained simply on their having been students there. I have always regretted that this idea, which would have made a splendid work for one branch of Deacon's work, fell through. The spirit of the time was against it. At any rate the Whig Government was. A decisive blow was given to it by the regulation that any schoolmaster admitted to Holy Orders thereby forfeited his Schoolmaster's Certificate." [7]

The college was opened in 1841 by the Rev. Derwent Coleridge, who possessed something of his kinsman's, S. T. C's vision, and he had a most remarkable influence on the men under his care. " For the first time, at least since the medieval glories of Oxford, a systematic attempt was being made to bring the higher education of the country into vital touch with the instruction of promising youths belonging mainly to the industrial and commercial classes.

" Much of the enthusiasm which has since been manifested on behalf of Elementary Education, or of Provincial University Colleges, or, as at the present moment, of schemes for University extension was, from 1841–1851, concentrated on the work which was being done at St. Mark's College. For churchmen there was the special interest which attached to an effort to show that within the limits of her own system, and by the use of her own appliances, the church could supply the discipline and training which was the confessed need of the teacher. We have, indeed, to pass onward a generation to the foundation of Keble College, to find a parallel for the ardour and the hope which the opening of St. Mark's College aroused among the Churchmen of 1841." [8]

Only a study of their domestic publications—histories, year books, magazines—and practical experience of their daily life, centred round chapel and common room, library, playing-field, and in the college clubs and societies, can show the spirit and life of the best church training college.[9]   They were and still are *almae matres* in a manner that no mere secular institution could be or ever is near to being: their old pupils speak of Derwent Coleridge or " Father John " (Rev. J. Menet, of Hockerill) with a peculiar love and venera-tion.   The difficulties of the church training colleges have always been on the material side—the raising of money to keep abreast of modern structural and technical requirements. A cheaper institution, the " day training college," rose up to rival the church's ideal, but it has almost gone.   " It further appears that every one of the Day Training Colleges, except the London Day Training College, has one or more Hostels attached to it.   There is apparently always a Hostel for women and the tendency is to provide Hostels for men also. The result is that by the provision of Hostels the Day Training Colleges are being transformed into residential Training Colleges, except for those students whose homes are situated in the immediate neighbourhood." [10]   No better proof could be found than that after long experience the advocates of the cheaper system have come to adopt that always followed by the church as being a necessary corollary to her conception of what the mind of the teacher should be.

The Newcastle Report [11] is a mine of information on the whole range of elementary education and it has some figures that may be quoted here, since the main provision of training colleges by voluntary effort had been completed by 1857, and later effort was concerned, as we have seen, in improving their quality rather than size or number.

Unfortunately the church's vision of a trained band of teachers inspired by high ideals depended for its proper realization on support from the state—the essence of the voluntary system after 1833 was that it was a partnership. But after 1861 and the introduction of the new code the Government defaulted—one college alone, St. Mark's, lost £800 p.a.[12] : as we have seen, Mr. Lowe did not care.

The history of the training colleges after 1870 was un-eventful, being happily little more than the evolution of the technique of training and a steady growth in the provision of buildings and apparatus, leading to a better standard of teaching, but subject to the limitations imposed by the Revised Code. The Training College Commission reported to the Archbishop in Nov. 1916 very fully on the property and material side generally of the church's training colleges : there were (p. 5)

12 men's colleges accommodating 1,276 students.
18 women's colleges accommodating 2,490 students.

30 colleges accommodating 3,766 students.

" The details are from figures specially supplied by the Board of Education . . . It appears that, including accommodation approved and now in course of provision, the total accommodation in training colleges for the training of Elementary Teachers in England and Wales is 12,482, so that whereas Church of England Training Colleges provide a total accommodation for 3,766 students, Colleges not connected with the Church of England provide accommodation for 9,076." " The voluntary Training Colleges not connected with the Church of England provide accommodation—

For men only   413
For women only   1,514
                   ─────
                   1,927 "

" In 1905 the Church of England colleges had accommodation for 3,755 students, while colleges not connected with the Church of England provided for 5,232. In 1895 the accommodation in Church of England colleges was 2,352, while all the other colleges taken together provided for 1,772. In 1890 all the recognized colleges were voluntary. The total accommodation was for 3,555, and Church of England colleges provided for 2,225 students." No increase in the numbers of denominational students was allowed by the Board of Education. Since 1890 the church's students have much increased, those of the other voluntary bodies much decreased, and the great increase in the number of students generally is due to provision by local bodies, including University training departments.

As a result of correspondence between the Archbishop of Canterbury and the president of the Board of Education, the Church Training Colleges were, in 1918, federated under a Board of Supervision and this body is recognized by the

Board of Education and has entered into working arrangements with it.

The year 1933 saw a further report—of the "Committee of Inquiry presented to the Board of Supervision of the Church's Training Colleges." By the previous year St. John's, Battersea, had been united with St. Mark's, Chelsea to form the College of St. Mark and St. John, and the Home and Colonial Society's College at Wood Green was closed. The result of this was no decrease in the number of church places in training colleges, for their numbers and resources were merely transferred. The two Welsh colleges were excluded from the Committee's report.

We must begin by saying that, although the work of the Church Training Colleges is to some extent comparable to that of the Universities, the financial burden involved in their maintenance at a level of efficiency required by modern conditions is far greater than that laid upon the authorities responsible for the Universities. To the latter through the Treasury the University Grants Committee makes direct grants in accordance with their needs, while the Church Training Colleges receive only capitation grants through the Board of Education. But this is not all, for the Board, regardless of the colleges' commitments for staff and accommodation expenses generally, varies the permitted number of students in accordance with the demand for teachers from time to time. In 1932–4 the students were reduced by 984, and this automatically reduced the grant to the 26 church training colleges by nearly £43,000, with possibility of a further decrease of £17,810.[13] All this was despite the fact that just previously the Board had asked colleges to provide an increased output of teachers in view of the possibility of Parliament's raising of the school leaving age and an alleged intention to reduce the size of classes. The colleges responded—and were left high and dry.

From 1921 the Church Assembly budget [14] has contained an item of £30,000 to £32,000 annually for religious education, and there have been considerable local contributions to the individual colleges, including many from former students, especially where diocesan ties are strong.

In addition great schemes of building have taken place. By the erection of new buildings at Chelsea at a cost of £50,000 it was possible to amalgamate the colleges of St. Mark and St. John. Whitelands was rebuilt on a new freehold at a cost of £150,000, and the new "Warrington" at Liverpool similarly cost £150,000. These are vast sums for voluntary effort and almost suggest the church's entry into the world of high finance.

" £10,000 was allowed for contingencies, and the monies required were raised by an issue of debentures secured upon (a) an annual sum provided in the Church Assembly Budget and (b) upon the new buildings. The amount required to amortise the capital was calculated to be £19,800 per annum for fifty years, and this sum is included in the Church Assembly Budget as a first charge." Large sums, not dependent on the current subscriptions of churchpeople, were with Parliamentary sanction borrowed from the Ecclesiastical Commissioners.

Finally, we append the numbers approved by the Board of Education, although this is generally well short of the accommodation available in the training colleges.[15] It was decided in 1937 to close three of the church training colleges —Peterborough, Brighton and Truro—and to distribute the places for which those colleges had been recognized amongst the other church training colleges.

In this essay no mention has been made of the foundation of Keble and Selwyn Colleges; of King's College, London; of Lampeter and the Theological Colleges. The story of Durham University has been told elsewhere by Canon Whiting and J. T. Fowler[17] and there is no necessity to detail it over again. But in this connexion it must be mentioned that the men at Bede College and the women at St. Hild's both have the opportunity of taking a Durham University degree to qualify for teaching in elementary or secondary schools, since these training colleges are " hostels " of the university. No mention will here be made of the halls of residence at Sheffield, Manchester and other universities, but some colleges not included under the previous heads may be noted.

Berridge House, West Hampstead we have already noticed in the history of the National Society as a Training College of Domestic Subjects: in 1938–9 it had 267 students in the year and the annual expenditure was about £31,000.

St. Christopher's College, Blackheath, for training leaders and teachers in the work of religious education in schools, dioceses and parishes had 34 students in 1940 and the annual expenditure was about £5,000 : it is closely connected with the National Society's Sunday school work. (The Sunday School

Institute was incorporated in the Central Council of Religious Education in 1936 : it had been founded as long ago as 1843.)

St. Mary's College in London was closed in 1940 and the students with their Principal and Staff joined St. Gabriel's College, Kennington, which has now been evacuated to Doncaster. Here the students of St. Mary's finished their course.

The Board of Education has now agreed to allow additional places at St. Gabriel's College for the training of Kindergarten teachers to take the place of those formerly trained at St. Mary's. These students will be prepared for the Higher Certificate of the Froebel Foundation and for certification by the Board of Education.

As in all enterprises largely controlled and financed by local effort, adequate statistics of the material support given to the church training colleges cannot be compiled. Even to-day some of these colleges are vested in the National Society, a diocesan board, or a private church trust, but they are federated under a Board of Supervision. What might have been accomplished had the Enabling Act been passed a hundred years ago we cannot tell, but centralized control has enormous advantages when combined with local supervision.

It will be clear that if the church's ideals and her control of the elementary schools have been overwhelmed by the developments for which municipal and government aid have been responsible, the same is not true of the training colleges. In the latter the church's practice of training future teachers by forming them into a community living a common life and seeking consecrated ends has never been challenged by a superior secular substitute. On the contrary, many young people to-day prefer the training college to the rather formless life which they would have to face, otherwise, in any save the ancient universities.

L. PARLIAMENTARY TRIBUTES TO THE CHURCH'S WORK

THE pages of Hansard are not a reliable primary source for the history of what the Church of England has accomplished for the education of the people, but the debates do help us to understand the story, and in a variety of ways.

The views of the political parties, of course, find expression in the House, but we meet nothing exceptional in these. Various shades of opinion in the country are also echoed, including the ideals and aspirations of the most progressive element. Qualitatively, the debates are interesting and valuable as a check on other evidence, but quantitatively they are very misleading. All members with a grievance air their opinions, real or fancied, and all minority views are vociferously expressed. There is an admirable forum for those who may wish to make political capital—always a fair number—out of questions of popular or any other kind of education, and especially for those who manage to pass off antipathy to the Church of England as zeal for popular education. But the pages of Hansard do not offer so much evidence of what has been solidly accomplished and approved by all men as they record criticisms of the past and alternative suggestions for the future.

The first quotation from Mr. Gladstone stresses two points that have arisen as major issues in this work—the representative character of the National Society and the vain efforts of the clergy to infect the laity with the same zeal and self-sacrifice for the cause of elementary education which they themselves had so generously exhibited.

Representative Character of the National Society and Lay apathy towards Popular Education.

Mr. Gladstone, 18th August, 1848.[1]

" Although arrangements with the National Society did not bind the Church, yet he might express a confident opinion, though without authority, that if the terms (of the management clauses)—modified as he believed they had been by the National Society, in order to meet the views of the Government—could be accepted by the Government, the vast

majority of the clergy of the Church of England at once,
and ultimately, he would venture to say, the entire clergy,
would be connected with the system that should be so agreed
upon between the Government and the National Society.
. . . He believed that, in nine cases out of ten, the complaint
of the clergy was, that they could not get the laity to take
interest enough in the management of the schools.   They
were anxious to court, not what was called interference—
that was an injudicious term and tended to prejudice the
case—but the assistance and co-operation of the laity in
carrying on these schools. . . . but if they could adopt
regulations by which in every case persons qualified, members
of the Church, that is, living in the actual use of the
ordinances of the Church, should be associated with the clergy,
a great benefit would be conferred on the Church, which
would be readily acknowledged by the clergy . . . a very
great increase of valuable assistance would be given to the
Church in the matter of education, and a very great benefit
conferred on the whole of the people."

(Sir G. Grey had previously remarked in regard to the
National Society " that he was not aware of any organ that
could be taken as a more satisfactory exponent " of the wishes
of members of the Established Church.)

Earl Russell.   March 8th, 1869.[2]

" . . . the complaint (of lay apathy in matters to do with
popular education) among the clergy is general.   They say
they cannot find willing subscribers among the land-owners,
and are obliged to contribute very largely in proportion to
their resources in order to keep up their schools.   I feel for
them, for I must say that the conduct of the parochial clergy
of the Church of England has been most admirable.   They
have subscribed to the utmost of their means for the promotion of education, solely, as I believe, from a desire to make
their parishioners better men and better Christians, and for
the general welfare of society.   Having thus exerted themselves, it is very hard that so great a proportion of the burden
should be cast on them."

Zeal of the Clergy for Popular Education truly Disinterested.
Mr. W. E. Forster in rising to move for leave to bring in his
Bill of 1870.[3]

" Now, while alluding to voluntary zeal, I must be allowed

to state that I think no one could occupy my office without being fully aware of what the country owes to the managers of the schools at present in receipt of Government grants. Both before and during my tenure of that office I have had many opportunities of seeing these gentlemen at work, particularly ministers of religion of all denominations, though perhaps it has been my lot to see more of the clergy of the Church of England than of others. I have seen them at their work, and tried to help them occasionally; I know the sacrifices they have made, and not for a moment do I believe it possible that any one who considers this question will disregard what they have already done, or will wish to do without their aid in the future. I sometimes hear it objected that they gain great influence by their work in promoting education. I believe that they have not worked in order to attain that object, though far distant be the time when, in England, self-denying exertions, such as many of these gentlemen have made, will not give them influence! " [4]

Mr. Beresford Hope.[5]

" Even the most pious Dissenter, in his own estimation, may learn a lesson of toleration from Archdeacon Denison—that man of vehement convictions, but broad forgiveness and chivalrous generosity. If the imputation, which has been scattered broadcast, shall be repeated, that Churchmen, and particularly the clergy, in supporting the Bill are influenced only by a sense of their own dignity, and the hope of ulterior personal advantage, there will be an end to the hopes of peace which are now bright about us." . . . " If the Church . . . wanted to trample on Dissenters . . . it would not welcome a Bill which will place every denominational school on the same level, no matter what the doctrine of the denomination may be, and no matter how incomplete the theological or classical education of its pastor. Under the secular system the Church would preserve its social prestige and its intellectual vantage ground; and, if its spirit had been such as the hon. and learned member for Stroud insinuates, it would have sided with the secular party."

We have to face the suggestion that the voluntary system by its inadequacy held up the progress of popular education. An ingenious advocate might possibly do something with this case, but he would have an exceedingly difficult task in explaining away the Revised Code of 1862. This was the deliberate creation of the Government, designed solely to reduce the amount of the education vote, regardless of the national welfare. There was thus no question of the state having ready a better alternative to the voluntary system. The Revised Code, in fact, held up the progress of popular education for a generation on the material side, and the evil legacy, a *damnosa hereditas,* of the Payment by Results system still remains.

Clergy, teachers, the National Society, all impartial observers, even Her Majesty's Inspectors, condemned this short-sighted and cynically reactionary measure carried out by Government.

Increased self-sacrifice and redoubled energy on the part of the clergy were necessary to counteract the niggardliness of the state.

The Revised Code's Adverse Effects on Popular Education and Increased Need for Clerical Self Denial.

Lord Robert Cecil, March 25th, 1862.[6]

Speaking on the motion for committee on the distribution of grants under the Revised Code.

" The peculiarity of the system was that the grant was not to depend on industry, but on a hundred other things—such as the impediments which might prevent the children attending school, the nervousness of the children, the temper of the examiner—with which the managers or teachers could have nothing to do, and for which, therefore, they could not be held responsible in the slightest degree. . . . but it should be recollected that the managers were poor men, clergymen in the receipt of small incomes, who would be utterly unable to bear the crushing weight the right hon. Gentleman proposed to place upon them. These managers, who were practically all clergymen with £200 or £250 a year, were asked to risk a sum equal to a sixth part or nearly a fourth of their income upon a scheme which made the risk depend upon such probable contingencies as the weather; or the attendance of either the child or the inspector, or the humour of the latter while performing his duties of examiner."

Mr. W. E. Forster, on the same.[7]

" A great proportion of the managers throughout the country were hard-worked and ill-paid curates, and these men, not infrequently, had to deny an education to their own children, while they discharged their duty in educating the children of the poor. When any of these managers had fulfilled all the costly conditions required by the state as to the means of teaching, he, of course, expected the state to pay the share it had engaged to pay. But what did the right hon. Gentleman say to him? He says, ' Here is a child of a poor man. You think it is your duty to educate him. I also think it is my duty, and therefore I will help you in this way. If at the end of the year you bring the child and prove to me he has been taught in a certain costly building, with certain costly apparatus, and by certain machinery also costly, by masters who I determine shall be costly, what do you expect?' The manager, of course, says, ' That you will pay me.' ' No,' says the right hon. Gentleman, ' I shall not pay you unless the child can do a certain amount of reading, writing and arithmetic: and not only that, but I will have your nine years old child up to the nine years old require-ments, and your eleven years old up to eleven years old requirements.' But the manager, in reply, says, ' I cannot do that, as a child of nine years old may come to me utterly untaught.' The right hon. Gentleman replies, ' I cannot help that; you ought to have got him before.' But the manager may add, ' I will keep him till twelve or thirteen, if you will allow me.' The right hon. Gentleman says, ' No, I will not pay you a farthing for him if you keep him after eleven, unless indeed he chooses to go to a night school '; to which he (Mr. Forster) was sure he was not at all likely to go."

Mr. Puller, on the same.[8]

" Many of the managers had been induced to undertake the work of education by the terms offered by the Govern-ment and now, after the lapse of fifteen years, when these parties had sunk their capital in bricks and mortar, had em-barked in a task necessitating considerable thought and anxiety, and had entered into contracts which could not be abandoned without mortification to themselves and disap-pointment and injury to others, they were told that the Government had changed their minds, and that, unless they could contrive under all circumstances, however different the circumstances might be, to come up to the requirements of the new Code they must go to the wall, and if they could not carry on their schools under the new scheme, they must shut up." [9]

H

Lord Robert Montagu on the Revised Code [10] had said that the Government's aim had been to help the voluntary system " to stimulate and help forward education.   This system existed in full force until it received a check from the present Chancellor of the Exchequer when he brought in his Revised Code.   He knew that the Revised Code had done a great deal of good in its way, but it certainly gave a check to the growth of schools and to the increase in the number of scholars.   The present Home Secretary had stated in that House in 1867 that—

" ' The Revised Code had aggravated one of the evils most strongly urged against our system—namely, that it gave aid where it was least wanted and withheld it where the need was sorest.' [11]

" The right hon. gentleman (Mr. Forster) ought, therefore, to complain of his colleague the Chancellor of the Exchequer and of the Government of Lord Palmerston, but for whom the number of schools would have increased more rapidly, and but for whom there would now have been no educational destitution.   It was true that the grants for education were then very large, reaching to nearly £1,000,000 sterling a year.   But that was partly because education was spreading so rapidly.   The object of the Revised Code was to decrease these enormous grants for education.   The present Chancellor of the Exchequer at the time himself stated that his object was to decrease that expenditure, and a decrease of expenditure meant a decrease in the means of supplying education. The right hon. gentleman in 1867, enamoured of the system to which he had given birth, had said—

" ' You are not contented, though the work is done better and cheaper (under the Revised Code).   You are not satisfied, but you must all begin tinkering and pulling to pieces the system which has produced such results.' " [12]

The Threat to the Voluntary or Non-Provided Schools.

Mr. W. E. Forster in rising to move for leave to bring in his 1870 Bill,[13]

" . . . we must take care not to destroy in building up— not to destroy the existing system in introducing a new one. In solving this problem there must be, consistently with the attainment of our object, the least possible expenditure of public money, the utmost endeavour not to injure existing and efficient schools, and the most careful absence of all encouragement to parents to neglect their children. I trust I have taken the House thus far with me. Our object is to complete the present voluntary system, to fill up gaps, sparing the public money where it can be done without, procuring as much as we can the co-operation and aid of those benevolent men who desire to assist their neighbours."

Lord Robert Montagu.[14]

" . . . they said they would see whether the people of England liked secular schools or not. The late Government were confident that the people of England preferred religious schools to secular, and so they determined to put both kinds upon an equal footing, to start them fair in the race, and prove that secular schools would not succeed. It was well known that the British and Foreign Society's schools, and even they belonged to the denominations and were by no means secular, had no hold on the country. The managers of these schools were religious men, the masters belonged to religious denominations, the Bible was read in the schools, but no catechisms or formularies were taught. The result was that this society had no hold on public opinion, and that the schools in which distinctive religious teaching was given were preferred by the people."

[15] " He was glad to hear that, in considering whether a parish was ' well supplied ' with schools, unaided schools were to be taken into account. For there were about 7,000 parishes now well supplied with unaided Church schools; while the schools of only 5,000 parishes received assistance from the State. Yet the former were excellent schools, inspected by the diocesan inspectors, and contained as many scholars as all the Dissenting, the Scotch, and the British schools under the Privy Council. The right hon. gentleman had alluded to dame schools. These were in most cases, at the time the Commissioners reported, inferior schools; and so the name acquired an opprobrium. But the case was very different now. In a parish of less than 100 inhabitants they could not have a large school, because the numbers were small, and the subscriptions were small. It was necessary, therefore, to have a cottage school, kept by some mistress, and under the immediate care of the clergyman of the Church of England. These schools were small in number, only 662, with 14,674 children, according to the National Society's

Report. These were not bad schools, and were confined to parishes in which there could be no other schools."

Mr. Gathorne Hardy,[16]

" Lord John Russell himself, in 1846, in bringing forward the Minute of Education, stated that it was the desire of Her Majesty that the youth of the country should be religiously educated, and that the rights of conscience should be respected. That was the foundation of the Bill as originally announced by the right hon. gentleman opposite (i.e. Forster). And what has been the effect of this statement? In 1847 a pamphlet was published called *The School in its Relations to the State, the Church, and the Congregation,* the author of which, I understand, is Sir James Kay-Shuttleworth, to whose exertions is due much of the progress we have made in education. The whole argument of that pamphlet was that an inseparable element of the organization of a congregation was a school. I know that no active, energetic and high-minded clergyman would deem his parish to be in a satisfactory state if he had not a school in connexion with his congregation, and if he did not teach the same truths to the children on week-days as he did to the adults on Sundays . . . efforts have been made by the clergy, who supposed that they had obtained a moral right to the assistance and countenance of the State, and if the grant were to be increased to others it ought also to be increased to them. I take, by way of illustration, a letter I have received from a clergyman who has been in Orders for a long time. He says—

" ' Thirty years ago I completed two schoolrooms for 300 children ; twenty-five years back I erected three rooms for boys, girls and infants—300—with teacher's residence ; in 1850, two others, with master's house, for 400 ; in 1867, three others, with teacher's house, for 500. I have no hesitation in saying that none of these would have been erected without my exertions. I have contributed to the whole more than £2,000. I have done this in good faith, trusting that the school deeds would never be violated.'

" In these cases religious instruction was given under the clergyman, and the managers were communicants. That gentleman has shown his zeal in the cause of education wheresoever he has gone. It would not be agreeable to him that I should mention his name, but he is an example of thousands of clergymen who take the deepest interest in these schools. Now it is most important not only that these schools should be maintained on the principle on which they were founded, and receive assistance from the State, but that they should not be sapped and put down by the establishment of rival schools. There ought to be a distinct understanding that the great efforts which have been made should be respected by the State, and that the State should do all it could to maintain the edifice it has helped to rear." [17]

II. THE CHURCH'S CONTRIBUTION TO SECONDARY EDUCATION

WHEN we left the Historical Introduction to this essay it was to study the church's contribution to something entirely new in English life—a systematic attempt to provide universal elementary education. We saw something vast and complex in the process of evolution, a system which to-day offers to every child in this country free schooling and compels those who do not accept the offer to provide themselves with some alternative form of primary education.

Very different is the history of secondary education,[1] and sharply contrasted in the problem it presented to the church in the nineteenth century. In the field of elementary education in the Victorian age the church struggled against those who had a different end in view. The state and dissenters were at different stages and in various ways setting themselves to create a kind of religious teaching, or an absence of it, to which the church could not agree. Again, the church was fighting against time, with the bogey of "educational destitution" ever in the background to keep the church's educational resources strained to the point of breaking. For if the voluntary system were clearly proved inadequate then it might be superseded—as it was, in fact, steadily superseded —by something far less satisfactory to the conscience of advocates of a real Christian education in the elementary schools of the country. (Not that this in character or technique was anywhere near ideal save in rare instances.)

In the secondary field, mainly a survival from pre-Reformation and Elizabethan times, competitors with an opposing ideology were almost unknown, and primary and secondary education in their very titles reflect, both in order and extent, the church's preoccupation with them.

"Secondary" is a very extensive term in education and is applied to a field of activity in which, to vary the metaphor, there are social strata whose extremes are very widely separated and whose needs are met (or whose prejudices are catered for) by schools forming nothing like a unified system.

We begin with the nine public schools[2] and their only slightly lesser fellows, nominally church schools, whether founded as great schools anciently or raised up by strong-minded headmasters. The Victorians really believed in these men and made their path easy, rewarding them handsomely and according them the highest status and prestige. This was all regardless of the fact that many headmasters of set policy took away the local grammar school from the people of the district and transformed it into a new public school for the benefit of the rapidly growing industrially enriched middle class of the country at large.[3] This was merely social climbing in the world of education.

Numbers of new public schools were also founded in a variety of ways, whose story may perhaps best be glanced at in the pages of the *Public Schools' Year Book*.

Both the great public schools and the less underwent profound changes, for which in fact as in legend the late Dr. Thomas Arnold, greater himself as schoolmaster than as churchman, was to a surprising degree responsible.

The conventional or Trollopian Church of England had nothing to fear from all this. The two universities until 1870 were in effect fully open only to anglicans, from thence came the schoolmasters, and the teaching of religion, by and large, was nearer church teaching than anything else. A few nonconformist public schools were seen to stand somewhat self-consciously among the rest, but it ended at that, and great numbers of dissenters sent their sons to English public schools: possibly a triumph of social over religious values and possibly an expression of the belief that the religious teaching could not possibly do their sons any harm. There were, it is true, tractarians and enthusiasts, but if the public schools produced such people, as they did, they had more sense than to be embarrassed by them. Thus for the upper middle-class and those above them the church had no need to bother; they were safe in the fixed tradition of loyal membership of the Established Church.

But the story does not end here. Victorian society was consciously ranged up and down a long social ladder and everybody wanted his place in the sun. Below the genuine public schools stood their substitutes, real and feigned. The former were often boarding schools of merit, run for private profit, that scrutinized with twin eyes the social origins and spiritual progress, more or less in accordance with the letter of the Prayer Book, of their charges. These, for a variety of reasons that are probably more amusing to us than discreditable to them, were for the most part strictly "Church of England." Parallel with them—and equally differing in their standard of merit—were schools conducted by boards of management with no desire to reap any financial advantage. There arose about the period 1845–70 a real demand for boarding schools, and these "proprietary" schools were often founded quite disinterestedly by churchmen to meet a genuine case of educational destitution, the patient prescribing his own remedy, in a particular class or district.[4] Where they were not church schools but were "connexional" the fact was widely known and constituted their chief appeal to zealots of the various denominations. All these were not what we should describe as *local* schools.

The local secondary schools were nearly always the grammar schools and were in a real sense schools for the people, and thus call for some notice here. Now great numbers of these, according to the evidence of the Schools Inquiry Commission of 1864–8 (Taunton), were in about the same state as Henry VIII's Commissioners would have us believe the English religious houses were in at the dissolution. They were seemingly past reform and their standard reflected the public interest, or lack of it, in secondary education. But in an age of clerical headmasters they were, if anything, church schools, though rather by tradition than conviction. Unfortunately, they were like the old Liberal Party, squeezed between the upper and the nether mill-stone. Some were glorified into public schools for the well-to-do and others were debased into national schools for the poor. For example, the "Endowed Grammar Schools at Frodsham and Bunbury" have become national schools and nothing more and have ceased to fulfil the intention of the founders. "The middle-class, it is generally admitted, is the neglected class. The rich endowments of the public schools and universities chiefly benefit the upper classes; the small grammar school is converted into a national school for the education of the poor."[5] This verdict is borne out by the evidence of the Schools Inquiry Commission. There was a real paucity of any save inferior private schools for farmers, tradesmen, and the "£10 householder class."[6] Our present state system of secondary education has evolved out of the elementary system, first alongside the old grammar schools and then inclusive of them, and in many ways is altogether admirable, but it had to wait until the elementary system itself had reached a

certain stage of development before it could be built up.
What the church did was to provide in various ways, directly
and indirectly, through its members, a vast amount of
educational provision for the middle-classes. The fact that
this was only a temporary provision does not diminish its
value for the age, and it was a necessary prelude to something
better.

We have noticed the very bad state of most of the ancient
local endowed schools, and it is noteworthy that when these
were given new " schemes " of government or otherwise re-
modelled, according to varying applications of the legal
doctrine of *cy près,* the episcopal visitors and *ex officio* clerical
governors tended to disappear and these schools began to lose
their " church " character.[7] Certainly in this respect founders'
intentions were often ignored or overridden as being invadi-
dated merely by reason of their antiquity.

This essay, however, is not concerned with the public
schools, since these can hardly be described as " popular,"
nor with the old endowed schools, since they date previously
to 1833. We cannot, nevertheless, pass them over entirely.
In their ideals and technique they have by a process of filtra-
tion given a legacy of inestimable worth to the state schools :
Arnold, Temple, Thring, Close, Prince Lee, Quick, Welldon,
Moss, Wilson—a vast catalogue of churchmen could be
readily compiled whose work made the state secondary
system possible. So great, in fact, has been their influence
over the state schools that the latter have often been too
zealous to imitate the great schools and have in consequence
been false to their special character and mission.

We must begin by saying that an exact estimate of the
church's provision of secondary education is quite impossible,
for the evidence does not exist. It came, of course, largely
under the head of " private enterprise " (to which category
we must assign all the Victorian and later public schools), as
contrasted with the Government " provided " or " aided "
schools, altogether apart from the fact that these early
secondary schools were not in a static condition as were the
elementary schools. Depending on their sensitivity to the
scholastic " market," these schools continually adapted themselves, as we see in the case of, say, the Woodard and Church
Schools Company's foundations and Cranleigh, and to-day
they often appear under very different forms. The most we
can attempt, therefore, is to give some details of those schools

that belonged to centralized groups, and indicate by example the varied types of individual schools set up all over the country, adding also that if the critic will make a careful survey of the history of the schools in any locality he will probably be surprised to see what provision for church children really was made.

Schools for the upper middle-classes—all this stratification is very rough and ready, but does correspond to certain facts —were chiefly boarding schools, and in themselves do not come within our scope. But they both set a fashion and gave expression to the belief that "boarding school" education was the ideal. Sewell's Radley, for example, must be left out, but we do not propose to be logical and exclude Lancing, since it formed an integral—in the literal sense—part of Woodard's scheme.

Now a distinguishing mark of the church's work for education has always been that it was a venture of faith in man and God and not merely the carrying out of routine provision, with boundless resources waiting to be tapped, as in the case of the state. Nowhere, perhaps, is this more clear than in the case of Nathaniel Woodard.[8] "The sixteen schools of the Woodard Corporation owe their collective existence and their name to an inconspicuous and poorly educated curate of ninety years ago, who faced the problem of middle class education as it stood at that day, and laid down the true lines of its solution. Others covered the same ground as he did so far as the upper middle classes are concerned; he stood alone in taking up, in addition, the championship of the lower." The story of Woodard's life and of his schools—for they are identical—cannot be told here, but one or two points may be made. Woodard faced literally incredible difficulties and had his failures—e.g. Leyton Military and Engineering School and the project for Lancing Tower—but he was a great realist. He was, too, as great a strategist as Sir Robert Morant and he knew the grades of the middle class with an insight given to few. "The nineteenth century approach to secondary education was obsessed by the idea of 'grading.' In 1868 the Schools Inquiry Commissioners (the Taunton Commission) spoke of 'grading' almost as their own discovery. But actually it was fully present in Woodard's mind twenty years earlier. The keen interest which the commissioners showed in the school which ultimately became Ardingly was due to the fact that it was the sole attempt in existence to organize a 'third-grade' school, not as a commercial gamble, but as a serious contribution to national needs." [9]   Woodard's acceptance of prevailing class distinctions has been condemned by unthinking persons of our day.   Woodard lived in a very different age, when to turn a blind eye to these facts was to court disaster.   He legislated with both eyes open to the realities of the situation.[10]

Woodard raised and spent vast sums, of which no record is available, but between the foundation of Shoreham school —the future Lancing—in 1847 and the year 1868 he had accounted for nearly a quarter of a million.   But this was only a start : Lancing chapel cost £300,000 [11] (and is still unfinished), and by 1887 nearly £100,000 [12] had been spent on Denstone alone.

The table in the notes [13] may give an idea of the magnitude of Woodard's achievement, and huge sums have been spent on the schools during the past twenty-five years, in order to bring them into line with the requirements of to-day.

In some ways comparable to the Woodard schools are those of the proprietory " Church Schools Company," founded in 1883, after a meeting at the National Society, as an anglican parallel to the Girls' Public Day School Trust.   They have had a chequered career, possibly because they left room for local control to take the schools, as local day schools, from the hands of the parent body.

By 1884 six schools had been established, 1885 saw four more, and in the years 1886–7 a further eight were set up. Altogether 34 schools have been founded in various ways at a cost to the company alone of only £65,000 the remainder being raised by local effort.   According to the jubilee publication—*Church Schools Company, 1883–1933*—seven schools [14] were under the company's control, and another fourteen had been handed over to local management.   All were inspected and recognized as efficient by the Board of Education, but were not state-aided.   There was thus no fear of the loss of religious liberty.

We may briefly say that rate- and state-aided schools were chiefly responsible for providing competition that some schools could not stand against and they had to close, but about 1,300 children are still being educated.   There are, of course, other Church High Schools : the *Official Year Book of the Church of England* [15] lists St. Mary's School, Lancaster Gate *(now*

closed) ; St. Margaret's, Bushey; Bournemouth and Grimsby
High Schools; while the Francis Holland (Church of England)
Schools Trust conducts two schools, educating 350 girls of
the middle and upper classes. It was founded in 1879. The
Church Education Corporation, founded in 1900 to establish
and maintain efficient secondary schools, runs three girls'
boarding schools recognized by the Board of Education, and
the *Official Year Book of the Church of England* also
mentions St. James' Secondary School at Grimsby, for 250
boys. This latter apparently resembles St. Augustine's
Grammar School, Dewsbury, in connexion with the Woodard
foundation, but owing to unfortunate local circumstances this
shared the fate of the Leyton school[16] : its life was in the
years 1884–1899.

There was much other work done of a purely local
character, where attempts were made to meet the needs of
a single district rather than to provide a large scheme, but
it is hoped that sufficient will have been done to suggest the
types of schools we may expect to find on studying particular
areas. There follow details of local secondary and the old
higher grade schools, and notes on some matters ancillary
thereto.

Canon J. L. Brereton[17] was a leader in a project to found
middle-class boarding schools to serve the district round them
and he was specially concerned with the " proprietary county
school " at West Buckland in Devon. This was founded in
1868 and by 1876 it had 150 boarders.[18] Other and similar
schools were not always so markedly successful. Companion
to it was an East Devon County School at Sampford
Peverell,[19] founded in 1860, and we may also note the North
Eastern County School at Barnard Castle.[20] The 1870–1
report of the Committee of Council[21] has a picture of the
Failand Lodge School, Somerset. It was started by clergy
and landowners for the children of the yeomanry and was
self-supporting. As many as 40 acres were taken on a 21
year lease (later renewed) and the sponsors put up the initial
cost of £600. It was a boarding school for 64 boys between
the ages of 7 and 15 years. " Doubtless the work and
excellence of the school are to be attributed in a great
measure to the unbought services of two neighbouring clergymen, who in turn spend two mornings each week with the
boys, being not uncommonly their instructors at other
times." [22] Similar to this was Weston Middle School,[23] while

the Rev. F. V. Thornton's School at Callington in Cornwall, which moved from Hampshire with its proprietor on his preferment, was a bold and successful effort.[24]

Cranleigh School[25] began as a proprietory county school for the local farmers' sons in 1865. Thirty years later the class it was intended to serve had disappeared, and it ceased to be a local school. It was a purely church school : similar was the very efficient (and still flourishing) St. Katharine's College, Bramley,[26] nearby, for girls. We may also note as typical Edgbaston Church of England College (1885);[27] King's Lynn High School for Girls;[28] Carshalton Church of England School for Girls;[29] Kelly College at Tavistock;[30] the Chantry School at Frome for girls, vested in the Bishop of the Diocese;[31] the Episcopal Middle School for Girls at Exeter.[32] Clapham School was founded in 1884 and had 145 pupils between 7 and 16 years old. It was run by the *Boys'* Public Day School Company.[33]

The impossibility of discovering the numbers either of " trust " (i.e. non-profit making schools), or private venture church schools is soon obvious to the student of this subject. A glance at the *Calendar of the English Church and Ecclesiastical Almanack, 1870* (Church Press Co.) besides public schools and endowed schools shows the following : (pp. 161–162) St. Peter's College, Rawdon, nr. Leeds—run by the incumbent—middle class school for boys and girls; on p. 108 is a mention of the Oxford Diocesan School, begun at Cowley in 1841; Devizes Proprietory Grammar School; Dorset County School,[34] St. Andrew's College, Chardstock, Dorset, founded under the special sanction of Bishop Hamilton on public school lines for the sons of gentlemen of limited means, is on p. 114, and finally (p. 115) St. Paul's, Stony Stratford. The 1895 Secondary Schools Report says (p. 381) that " Liverpool College School . . . is one of four Church of England Schools, founded by the same company, and managed by the same Council, under the name of the Liverpool College. The schools are of three grades; they are called ' Upper, Middle and Commercial ' respectively, and are all boys' schools. The girls' school was established in 1856, and was the only public girls' school of the first grade in Liverpool, till . . . 1881."

This brings us to the North of England, where the schools tended to be larger and more inclusive. We may notice Bolton Church Institute in some detail for the light it throws

on some of these Northern efforts. The Institute set out to
" provide a classical and commercial education in conformity
with the principles of the Church of England." It had three
departments—

I   Boys (121 pupils)
II   Girls (87 pupils) and Kindergarten (17 children)
III Evening Classes (in 1891–2, 823 students)
(run in partnership with the School Board).

We are told that " the fees are distinctly less than those of
the grammar school, and, as the advantages are equal, and
in the matter of laboratory in favour of the Institute, the
greater numbers of the Institute are accounted for." [35]   In
every way the Bolton Church Institute was regarded as
" enlightened " [36]—like so much Lancashire Churchmanship.
Note is made [37] of the great work of an ex-principal, the
Rev. J. W. Cundey, for Bolton's School Board and education
generally. A real effort was made to keep up the large and
extraordinary heterogeneous collection of proprietory, private
and other schools which the church recognized as her
secondary provision of education to a satisfactory standard
of scholastic attainment. The " local examination " system,
out of which has evolved the School and Higher Certificate
Examinations so highly prized in most quarters to-day, had
its origin in a characteristic piece of " voluntary " action.
The Aclands—a famous west country family of churchmen—
furnished a pioneer who wrote and worked carefully for
secondary education, especially for the county and middle
schools. " An enlightened and benevolent man, Mr. (later
Sir Thomas Dyke) Acland,[38] had been for some time planning
and fostering public examinations and prizes in connexion
with Middle Schools; but the good he had brought about
would have died with him, if not before, had it not been for the
judicious and successful advice of Mr. (Archbishop Frederick)
Temple, who has got the middle school examinations attached
on to those deep-rooted and stable bodies, the Universities,
thus securing for them a permanent character and position."

Our next subject is the provision of schools of the " commercial " type, and here we may conveniently begin with the
work of the National Society. We find it (p. 22 above)
unable to help the " middle " school at Leeds, but we have
seen the setting up of its Middle Class School Committee.[39]
It was fated from the very nature of things to accomplish

but little. The public and proprietory boarding schools at one end of the scale men knew, and the elementary schools at the other, but few people cared for these " higher grade " schools : [40] private enterprise generally filled the gap.

It may be interesting to see what the National Society's committee had accomplished in 1871. The details of schools related to the committee are really more important for what they reveal on the negative rather than on the positive side : the schools swept into the net are an extraordinary assortment.[41]

Apart from schools in union with the National Society's Middle Class Schools Committee the society had a direct hand in founding middle schools.[42] At York there was a middle school, chiefly for the sons of farmers, called the Yeoman's School and run in connexion with the York Training College for teachers. It was later merged in Archbishop Holgate's Foundation.[43] In being connected with a training institution it resembled St. Mark's College Upper School, established in 1841, which fifty years later had 346 pupils between 7 and 15 years of age.[44] At Lichfield there was a diocesan commercial school, and National Society middle schools existed at Canterbury, Lincoln, Chester and elsewhere.

The Church Extension Association, founded in 1865 and incorporating the Education Union, set up a large middle class school, the Old Palace School, at Croydon in 1889 : [45] in 1894 it established, at Liverpool, Sefton Park High School for Girls.[46] We have already noticed the Middle Class School at Leeds,[47] and the Rev. Robert Gregory (later Dean of St. Paul's, the Treasurer of the National Society) as a Lambeth incumbent ran a higher grade school for about 100 boys.[48] As an administrator Dean Gregory, therefore, had had practical experience of actual schools, as had the Rev. J. C. Wigram,[49] an advantage shared with these officials of the National Society, surely, by no one at Whitehall in their day. We have the evidence of a small tradesman who had a son at Mr. Gregory's school and another son at Woodard's St. Saviour's, Shoreham : both he and his friends believed in the real value of church education and were prepared to make definite sacrifices to secure it. It would be unfair to generalize from this witness's evidence, but this authentic testimony of a member of the class for whom the schools were provided is interesting and convincing.[50]

The parochial clergy of St. Pancras[51] founded and conducted a quite well-known school, the North London Collegiate School, to educate " the respectable middle classes," which had a very good academic record. It seems clear that some National schools became in fact middle or higher grade schools, although not classed as such by official nomenclature : Abbot's Ann may be cited as an example. The evidence of the headmaster of St. Thomas', Charterhouse, Schools explicitly stated that he had been specially allowed to run his Upper school in conjunction with the National Schools.[52] And the Rev. Wm. Rogers gives in his *Reminiscences* details of the middle schools he set up after leaving St. Botolph's, a city parish.[53] At Liverpool, St. Martin's Commercial School was an upper school for the middle classes,[54] and when the Granby Row School, Manchester was visited by Her Majesty's Inspector he was accompanied by the inspector of the Manchester Church Education Society, under whose care the school was.[55] Another similar school was also visited.[56] The Society had " made a recommendation to establish " four commercial middle schools " for one portion of the population —namely, the middle class, for which scarcely any public education is provided in the parish " in 1845,[57] and promptly acted upon it.

The Rev. Francis Close of Cheltenham, later Dean of Carlisle, founded a Cheltenham Trade School for Girls,[58] but it was the Bristol Trade School that acquired real fame in its day. The Bristol Diocesan School was in 1853 superseded by National Schools and the Committee wrote to the Rev. Hy. Moseley, H.M.I. for advice. The Inspector suggested a new kind of technical or trade school for former pupils of the National Schools, a higher grade school, " the crown of the elementary school system." It was opened in 1856, by the Lord President of the Council. The qualifications for admission were a knowledge of reading and writing, and the first four rules of arithmetic, simple and compound.[59]

There was a sliding scale of fees : for sons of artisans, 4d. per week; for sons of tradesmen, 6d. ; others paid one shilling. The same principle was applied to the lessons on chemistry, mechanics and natural science.

Now this school had a unique feature. In classical schools there was one central subject to which the rest of the curriculum was subservient, and here it was experimental science to which everything was carefully related. English is often a weakness in technical schools, but pains were taken to keep a good standard. Great stress was laid on all forms of practical work : geometrical drawing related to industrial processes and work in the laboratory. Much opposition was encountered from parents—not to the daily prayers and the visits of an honorary chaplain to open the day with a Bible lesson—but to the teaching of Euclid ! Much homework was done and the number of boys, originally 60, soon became 107—and the figure rose. There was a bracing intelligent atmosphere about the school that was specially noticeable, and the pupils' notes were a model of neatness. The staff in their own way were specialists. The school catered for boys of the lower middle class, and its success was chiefly attributed to the integration of the curriculum round such a practical subject as experimental science. The school won more prizes under the Science and Art Department than any other in England, while the evening schools compared with those of Manchester and Liverpool. A close connexion with Bristol trade was maintained and the best scholars were sought after as apprentices.

So much for the provision of secondary education where the church's teaching was an essential part of the school's curriculum. The church is not committed to any particular kind of education, whether elementary or secondary, any more than she is theoretically tied to the support of any particular kind of political system : the church's sole criterion is the citizen's right to live the Christian life. Consequently we may in this context describe as church schools a vast assortment of institutions with widely different aims and methods, all having little or nothing in common save that their religious teaching was in accordance with the principles of the Church of England, and to-day these in their hundreds range from Eton and Winchester to the smallest private venture preparatory school. Yet they have, for the most part, no official ties with the church.

It is well to remember that the tendency of the state practice to-day to keep the secondary schools of a monotonously uniform type, comprising still some of the old elementary school defects, is in no way due to the church, which has at any rate avoided the evils of standardization.

As things are at the moment, what is chiefly required in state secondary education is the infusion of the specifically Christian element that the church alone can give. The extraordinary power and value of totalitarian education may be

I

seen in Germany to-day, though used as the instrument of
evil purposes. What could be achieved by a properly
applied Christian philosophy of the inter-related man, society
and God we can only vaguely wonder at, for it is part of the
authentic vision of the Kingdom of God.

III.   CRITICISM AND SURVEY

THE writer who sets out to claim that contemporary thought on the subject of the church's contribution to popular education does not always square with the facts has indeed undertaken a difficult task. An enormous amount of research on the subject of education, it may be retorted, has taken place in the last quarter of a century.   Some of the acutest minds in the country have been eagerly engaged in helping forward both the theoretical and practical sides of this great national, nay international, activity: how then can a single worker in this field claim to establish his case that current views on anything save the tiniest detail are in need of re-orientation? Such a claim, it may be argued, must have a two-fold basis, the discovery of new material of such a kind as to require a modification of existing historical judgments or the postulating of a new approach to the old evidence.

The following quotation may be cited,[1] partly to act as a judge of the merits of sharply contrasted cases and partly to stand as an advocate of one side.   "Once again one is impressed by the fact that the Bell and Lancaster Societies, which became the National Society and the British and Foreign School Society, representing respectively the Anglican and Nonconformist Churches, stood in the way of State Education very directly for at least seventy years.   It perhaps is not fair to judge their outlook of a hundred years ago from a present day standpoint, but it is easy to see now that if the Churches had agreed to concentrate on the giving of Christian religious teaching, and to leave the State to manage secular education, we should have marched steadily ahead instead of wandering in the wilderness all those years." It would be quite difficult to find a reputable writer crowding so many misconceptions into a single paragraph, and a return will be made to this later for criticism.

In the opening sentences reference was made to the necessity of producing either new material or, if the old sources of evidence are to be used, of formulating a new critical approach.   The case is that something of both has been achieved.

Material and Sources

Our main sources are the domestic records of the National Society—its minute books, 1833–39, in the formative years; its annual reports, and, above all, its periodical surveys of the state of church elementary education. Partly, no doubt, because of their inaccessibility it is hard to find any printed reference to them even singly. Taken as a body, it is safe to say that no printed work has made any attempt to include them all in its compass. The 1846–7 survey made by the National Society, with the aid of a grant from Parliament, may well be claimed as a source for the wider field of English social history: its value lies far beyond the narrower range of the field of education. It may, indeed, be put forward as in part a corrective to the work of Engels on the state of the English working-classes in the year 1844.

All this, as it were, is on the positive side: on the negative may be set the claim that the usual sources for nineteenth century educational history must come in for criticism. The reports of the Committee of Council are valuable, and they have always been read side by side with those of the National Society, each supplementing the other,[2] but the generality of writers on the history of education, misled, no doubt, by the great reliability of Government statistics to-day, have attributed to them an accuracy and an all-embracing character and purpose that they certainly did not possess before the year 1918.[3] Government statistics of the achievements of the church in the field of elementary education in the nineteenth century are, then, entirely inadequate; which writers have turned to the church's records to implement them? Another point in connexion with the records of the Committee of Council, the Board of Education, Select Committees and Royal Commissions is that the present writer claims to be the first to have read them not with a *general* view but with a *church* view, deliberately noting the church's varied contributions through the century and later. And although much may be said in favour of the judicial mind of Select Committees and Royal Commissioners, yet even these have a remarkable tendency to produce reports which, whether majority or minority, might have been forecast from the previously known convictions of their members![4]

We close this section with the suggestion that of all the different aspects of popular education that have received the attentions of modern experts, the historical has been, proportionately, most neglected. If we take away the names of Frank Smith, J. W. Adamson, F. Birchenough and G. A. N. Lowndes we remove much of the best work done in this field.

Critical Approach

In dealing with " sources " the ground is fairly safe for they are tangible and susceptible of more or less exact treatment. But what in the present instance is labelled " critical approach " is a much more subjective and debatable matter, and the approach must be guided by strictly historical principles.

In all criticisms of what the church did or did not achieve the criterion must be a contemporary criterion and not an anachronistic one of to-day. We have no right to interpolate the " ifs " of history and the standard of comparison must be only what was fairly to be expected at the time.

This, for example, when applied to the volume of education actually being provided by the church in 1870 involves a number of important factors. There is primarily the economic factor, so often neglected and so often now stressed as of paramount importance. What financial resources had the National Society, the clergy, and the laity at their disposal? Then, as critics of the church so often forget, there were two sides to the provision of elementary education : on the one hand, the church had to provide the accommodation in the first place and to maintain it; on the other hand, the parent had to be able to afford to send his child. Apart from any fees, could the parent even afford to neglect the child's potential contribution to the slender family budget? The low standard of nineteenth century elementary education, it may be claimed, is very closely related to the popular standard of living, that mass poverty which persisted for so long, to become an economic factor entirely beyond the church's control. Further, we in this present age are in some respects wiser after the event in our criticisms.

By no means all intelligent men of good-will were convinced in 1870 that universal elementary education was undoubtedly " a good thing " : to-day, because of 70 years of experimental proof, no one doubts it. In assessing, again, the church's contribution in 1870 there must be reckoned the fact that since 1833 at least the church had been making a venture of faith that was opposed by disinterested men whose opinions were respected. Any one who has been a W.E.A. tutor will know what is meant when it is said that the church had to create the demand for popular education and then to supply the need.

This is only part of the picture. To-day it is known that, if it is not ideal, it is workable to provide what is in effect a purely secular education under the state system: in 1870 this solution to the problem of religious teaching seemed to many a leap into the abyss.[5] The Victorian age had grievous faults (nor is our own free from equally serious, if different, faults) but it was essentially a *theological* age: our own, by contrast, is a *humanistic* (or *scientific?*) age. In assessing what the church did for education this radical distinction must ever be borne in mind by the historian, otherwise criticism may be misdirected.

Unless, then, these objective economic factors and subjective religious influences are properly appreciated the picture may be misread, and the present writer seriously claims that a lack of understanding of what religion meant to these Nonconformists and Tractarians and Roman Catholics and churchmen generally prevents many people from seeing things in the right perspective.[6]

Before examining the validity of this claim it may be well briefly to account for the fact that so many modern writers on the history of education betray a complete lack of appreciation of what is meant by religion. To-day we are witnessing that religious " indifferentism " which the early Victorian clerical educational pioneers prophesied would come under a secular system of state education. If this " indifferentism " is applied to subsidiary questions, such as church " order," we shall not really complain, but when it covers such fundamental issues as the Incarnation itself, with all its moral and sociological implications, we have a duty to be anxious. Vast numbers of technically well-educated people have not the slightest understanding of the Christian religion. All that vast number of persons educated in the state elementary and secondary schools, at London and all the provincial universities, have normally no formal religious teaching as part of their education, nor any experience of institutional religion.[7] Thus as they meet the religious factor they are, like the rest of us, inclined to dismiss as irrelevant what they do not understand. One final point: the present writer claims that only those of the household of faith can really and to the core properly appreciate the mind and motives of those who built up Christian education in our land during the last century,[8] and without this understanding they cannot begin to be sympathetic critics of what the church both achieved and failed to achieve.

Perhaps it is now time to deal with Sir Percy Jackson's various statements. First as to the charge that the voluntary societies stood in the way of state education very directly for seventy years. This must refer to the period 1833–1902. What is the truth during those years about the state's activity? It is that Parliament had little interest in education and was in the position, until 1870, of a mere subscriber to the voluntary societies at first and then latterly to the individual voluntary schools. Nor is it true to say that the voluntary system was a check on the activity of the state. Two points here may be made: the Newcastle Commissioners only expressed the opinion of the country when they reported that they were against any diminution of the state grant and equally against state interference in education[9]—the plain fact was that public opinion did not desire a Government scheme of education. There was no question of the voluntary system barring the way to something better. Our second point is that the position was the reverse of this and the proud handiwork of Lowe and Lingen deliberately sabotaged the progress of English education. The Revised Code was a major disaster both for the teachers and the children:[10] it was an attempt, cynically indifferent to the welfare of all concerned, to save the taxpayer's pocket and the taxpayer acquiesced in it. The position did not radically improve in the years immediately after 1870, for great pressure had to be brought on very many parents to send their children to school at all. The plain truth is that it was all in accord with English tradition and experience that the voluntary principle in education, as in so many other things, had to come first and prove itself before the state could take over. And in the more spiritual aspects of education many observers of to-day can see that the state system has serious deficiencies that are not in its power of itself to supply.

There is no need to stress again the fact that the last century must be judged by its own standards, but there is some worth in the statement that the state might have provided the secular instruction and "the churches" the religious. But the church distrusted, and with reason, the state and quite rightly fought against being reduced to the level of one amongst many competing sects. Such a solution, in the vastly changed atmosphere that we have to-day, many of us look for in the future, through "Agreed Syllabuses," and concerted action by groups of Christian bodies.

There is one further detail to clear up. The theologian means by "the church," both the clergy and the laity, but secular writers have a habit of attributing the failures of "the church" solely to the clergy. By their own definition, "the church" has a simply magnificent record in the huge volume of clerical effort and self-denial for the sake of the elementary education of their country's children, which really forms the keynote of the whole story.

To conclude: "Whatever the future may bring forth, it must always be a subject of pride that the Church of England has done her duty to the children committed to her charge, in the face of popular indifference and national neglect." [11]

NOTES

HISTORICAL INTRODUCTION TO 1833

[1] A masterly study is by Bishop Hensley Henson: *The Church of England* (1939). Chapter VIII, pp. 185 ff., deals with Education.

[2] Cyril Norwood: *The English Educational System* (1928), pp. 9–10.

[3] Cathedral Chapters had a threefold responsibility: the *opus Dei*, education, repair of the fabric. (See esp. *Report of the Schools Inquiry Commission*, 1868: Memorandum on Cathedral Schools by C. J. Elton in Vol. VII, pp. 637 ff. This is wrongly stated on the "Contents" page as 673.)

[4] See esp. Allen and McClure: *Two Hundred Years—The History of the S.P.C.K.*, Chapter IV, pp. 135 ff. Also p. 50 for the London Charity School Trustees. These were formed from the S.P.C.K. but separated in 1868.

[5] E.g. the Rev. Thos. Stock, Rector of St. John Baptist, Gloucester.

[6] Quoted with approval by the Rev. Rd. Burgess, *Letter to the Rev. W. F. Hook, D.D.*, p. 5. It may be as well to make it perfectly clear that "prior to 1918 the Board had no means of ascertaining the number or size or character of schools not in receipt of grants." (Sir L. A. Selby-Bigge: *The Board of Education*, p. 24.)

[7] For the unsatisfactory nature of the 1833 Census of Scholars by the Secretary of State for the Home Department, see *Nat. Soc. Annual Report, 1835*, pp. 15–16. For a criticism of Lord John Russell's census figures of 1838 see Appendix I. A clerical enthusiast for education who acted as a sort of voluntary part-time inspector, the Hon. and Rev. Baptist W. Noel, shows a far smaller number of pupils in attendance at school than that reported by the Manchester and Birmingham Statistical Societies' report on Birmingham, Manchester, Liverpool and other Lancashire towns. (*Comm. of Council Report, 1840–1*, pp. 158–88, esp. Appendix, Table II, p. 179.) See also the state of affairs revealed by the Rev. John Allen, H.M.I., in the mining districts of Durham and Northumberland (*ibid.*, pp. 125–53).

[8] Manchester Statistical Society, quoted by the Report of the Select Committee on the State of Education, 1835, Appendix, pp. 101 ff. See this Report, and that of 1834, especially evidence of the Rev. W. Johnston and the Rev. J. C. Wigram for the work of the National Society and of Mr. Henry Dunn and others for the British and Foreign School Society. See also Sir Jas. Kay-Shuttleworth; *Four Periods of Public Education*, 1862, pp. 3–84: "Condition of Manchester in 1832." He would be a bold man who would claim that any school system could progress in such a state of affairs.

[9] *Comm. of Council Report, 1841–2*, pp. 273–4.

[10] The educational ideals of the National Society are given in Appendix III.

[11] E.g. the Hon. and Rev. B. W. Noel, a keen promoter of schools who admitted all denominations and "imposed" no anglican teaching. (See his evidence in the Select Committe Report of 1835, pp. 59 ff.) Similarly the Home and Colonial School Society, founded in 1836, was an anglican society that educated all comers and exacted no pledges from local committees of school managers. The Rev. R. H. Quick when at Sedbergh

resigned his chairmanship of the church school managers as a protest against their continuing the appointment of what he considered an inefficient head teacher and transferred his interest to the local British school. (*Life and Remains of the Rev. R. H. Quick,* p. 96. Ed. by F. Storr, 1899.)

[12] See Mathew: *Catholicism in England, 1535–1935,* a stimulating and balanced study.

[13] The Wesleyans insisted on teaching the necessity of " conversion."

I. THE CHURCH AND ELEMENTARY EDUCATION

A. The Constitutional Position of the Church of England in 1833

[1] For opposition to the revival of convocation reference may be made to Warre Cornish: *English Church in the Nineteenth Century,* Vol. II, pp. 33 ff. There was even a " Society for the Revival of Convocation." (Biber, *Life of Bp. Blomfield,* p. 389.) For the whole period, see N. Sykes: *Church and State in England in the Eighteenth Century* (1934).

[2] Opposition came from Queen Victoria, Prince Albert and the Court, most of the leaders of the political parties, the press (save on occasion *The Times*) and much of the populace, apart from the Roman Catholics and Protestant Nonconformists! " The Prince Consort recorded his own opinion in a formal memorandum to the Prime Minister that no Crown preferment was to be conferred on a Tractarian: thus, he explained, abler young men would be deterred from accepting their opinions. The policy was followed, but it did not bring about the desired result." (S. L. Ollard and F. L. Cross: *Anglo-Catholic Revival in Outline,* p. 35.)

B. The Church School in the Parish

[1] The Madras or monitorial system of Bell and Lancaster allowed a teacher to concentrate on a few children at the top who in turn taught those below them. These, again, instructed others and so on down the educational ladder.

[2] Nat. Soc. Monthly Paper No. LII, of April, 1851, p. 121. (For " a schoolmaster of the old style in Devonshire," Roger Giles, " Surgin, Parish clark and Skulemaster, Groser and Hundertaker," (P.S.—I tayches gografy, rithmetic, cowsticks, jimnasticks, and other chynees tricks)," see S. Baring-Gould, *The Vicar of Morwenstow, being a Life of Robert Stephen Hawker,* new and rev. ed., 1899, pp. 151–2.) A useful picture is given by the Rev. M. C. F. Morris, *The British Workman—Past and Present* (1925), pp. 5 ff., of an old schoolmaster, with other interesting material.

[3] Nat. Soc. Monthly Paper, No. LII, of April, 1851. Italics quoted.

[4] Richd. Dawes: *Schools and other similar Institutions for the Industrial Classes,* 1853, p. 20.

[5] For this survey see pp. 40 ff. The pages are not numbered. The general conclusion on this point is borne out by the Reports (on a much smaller scale) of Her Majesty's Inspectors in the several Reports of the Committee of Council, e.g. 1845, Vol. I, pp. 279–323, where comments are given on individual schools, many of them being of high character.

[6] For the state of affairs here see the Comm. of Council Report, 1841–2, p. 156—Report of the Rev. John Allen on the state of several schools in the County of Derby.

[7] Quoted in J. L. and B. Hammond, *Lord Shaftesbury* (Pelican Edn.), p. 78. House of Lords, 12/7/1842.

[8] See *Questions answered by Mr. Dicker, etc.* As against this see Allen and McClure: *Two Hundred Years,* p. 138. In the year 1704—The Master to teach the boys " the true spelling of Words, and distinction of

Syllables, with points and Stops " and also to write " a fair legible hand with the grounds of Arithmetick."

[9] Comm. of Council Report, 1861–2, p. 75.

[10] Nat. Soc. Annual Report, 1858, p. xi.

The figures quoted are for schools in DIRECT *union only with the National Society.*

	Sunday and Daily Schools.	Sunday Schools.	Sunday and Daily Scholars.	Sunday Scholars.
1846–7.	6,798	1,597	526,754	237,848
1838.	4,581	2,197	346,346	253,012
	+ 2,217	— 600	+ 180,408	— 15,164

[11] Nat. Soc. Monthly Paper, No. VII, of July 5th, 1847.

[12] *Memoirs of Early Life,* p. 19.

[13] Comm. of Council Report, 1845, p. 226.

[14] E.g. at Ewelme, Oxon., this is explicitly the case.

[15] Comm. of Council Report, 1841–2, pp. 309–10. See also Newcastle Commission (1858 : Report, 1861), Vol. II, p. 132–7 : " Table showing the Sources of Voluntary Contributions." The entry " Deficiency made up by the clergyman " is very common and we meet " Cost entirely borne by the rector, who also built the schoolroom " as quite consonant with the context.

[16] *On rendering more Efficient the Education of the People,* 1846, p. 7.

C. THE EARLY YEARS OF THE NATIONAL SOCIETY

[1] Nat. Soc. Annual Report, 1838, p. 13. For the work of the National Society prior to 1833, see statistics of its progress in 1819, 1826, 1832, in the Select Committee Report of 1834, pp. 138–9.

[2] For Terms of Union with the National Society, see Appendix II.

[3] Nat. Soc. Annual Report, 1836, p. 11.

[4] Nat. Soc. Annual Report, 1835, p. 13. The Library of the National Society contains many individual reports of these associations.

[5] *Ibid.,* p. 15.

[6] Nat. Soc. Annual Report, 1836, p. 61. " Summary of the Diocesan and District Societies and Schools in Union " gives lists of societies with statistics of pupils. But in addition to this quantitative information a qualitative survey is made of large numbers of former pupils, to test the efficacy of the character training received in schools. It is claimed that such a survey had never previously been made.

[7] Nat. Soc. Annual Report, 1835, p. 12.

[8] Text in Nat. Soc. Monthly Paper, No. XXXV, of November, 1849.

[9] Nat. Soc. Annual Report, 1856, p. xxxi, Appendix VI.

[10] See also the Newcastle Report, Vol. I, pp. 57–8, for a Table of Expenditure, etc., of the diocesan boards, 23 of them, in 1858. Their income was between £13,000 and £14,000. It is noteworthy that Durham, the first board, was founded as early as 1811.

[11] Biber : *Life of Bp. Blomfield,* p. 267.

D. THE CONFLICT OF CHURCH OPINION ON THE ELEMENTARY EDUCATION QUESTION

[1] Birchenough : *History of Elementary Education,* 1st Edn., 1914, p. 90, note, says that Kay-Shuttleworth was a Nonconformist. He later corrects this in his 3rd edn. See also Prof. Frank Smith's *Life of Sir James Kay-Shuttleworth,* pp. 81–2, for a footnote summary of his religious convictions, which were the dynamic of his work.

[2] G. A. Denison: *Position and Prospects of the National Society*, 1853, p. 7.

[3] *Memoirs of Sara Coleridge*, Vol. I, p. 213.

[4] Churton: *Memoir of Joshua Watson*, 2nd edn., p. 229.

[5] Nat. Soc. Monthly Paper, No. LXVIII, of July, 1852, p. 194.

[6] The Rev. Ed. Girdlestone was also concerned in this agitation, but it is significant that a memorial against it signed by 77 resident members of the Senate of the University of Cambridge was sent to the National Society. (Nat. Soc. Monthly Paper, No. LXVI, of May, 1852, p. 130.)

[7] Biber: *Bp. Blomfield and His Times*, p. 266. This society was instituted in May, 1853. Its supporters were men like Canon Hugh Stowell (see J. B. Marsden: *Memoir of the Life and Labours of Canon Hugh Stowell*, 1868). It made grants to schools and for the training of individual teachers. By 1858, according to its Fifth Annual Report, its annual income was under £3,000, but the Newcastle Commission Report, 1861, Vol. I, p. 575, gives the income as only £1,782.

[8] For Rd. Burgess, see the *D.N.B.* The quotations that follow are from his pamphlet *Educational Statistics*, 1838, a particularly penetrating analysis.

[9] See Prof. Claude Jenkins' brilliant lectures, *Frederick Denison Maurice and the New Reformation*. The third lecture, pp. 61–86, deals with the subject of education.

[10] *Has the Church or the State the Power, etc.*, p. 163.

[11] Cf. the Rev. W. G. Peck, of the Industrial Christian Fellowship in *Social Implications of the Oxford Movement*, p. 322. " It seems that once again the Church will have to undertake the task of directing the very motive and conception of education. An industrial era has provided us with a false substitute for education in that it has employed the schools to fit our youth for ' earning a livelihood,' as though that were the supreme response of an immortal soul to the wonder of the Universe. The generations to come will need to be educated for life: for life which will offer them in overflowing measure the perilous gifts of personal freedom, material sufficiency, and time which they may call their own."

[12] *On the Means of Rendering More Efficient the Education of the People—A letter to the Lord Bishop of St. David's*. 1846. 9th Edn. (All in 1846.)

[13] *Ibid.*, p. 6.

[14] See pp. 40 ff. for the Nat. Soc. survey.

[15] *loc. cit.*, p. 11.

[16] *Ibid.*, p. 12.

[17] E.g. Canon R. C. Clifton: *A Letter to the Rev. Dr. Hook*, 2nd edn., no date, p. 3—" You are known to be an earnest and practical man of almost unequalled activity in the discharge of your very responsible duties as a Parish Priest, labouring most energetically and successfully in your ministerial office in one of the most populous and influential districts in England."

[18] Nat. Soc. Monthly Paper, No. VIII, of Aug. 5th, 1847, pp. 4 ff. " Digest of Reports of Local Boards."

[19] The Society's initial difficulties and the success of its work are seen in the following extracts.

A teacher: " I am come to look on, Sir. I cannot stay but I should like to see a little. I have been a schoolmaster many years, and I cannot commence learning again."

The leader's Comment: " These very masters, in the course of a day or two, would be found sitting in the class, and answering questions as eagerly as the youngest." *Ibid.*, No. IX, of Sept., 1847. There is a list of 92 masters attending evening classes, *ibid.*, No. XIV of Jan. 31st, 1848.

[20] Nat. Soc. Monthly Paper, No. XXVII, of March, 1849, p. 28.

Name of Institution.	Period of Training	Numbers sent out.					
		1843	1844	1845	1846	1847	Total.
St. Mark's, Chelsea. (Masters.)	3 yrs.	3	11	18	23	19	74
Battersea Institution. (Masters.)	1 yr.	—	1	24	36	50	111
Westminster Institn. (Masters.)	6 mths.	74	93	84	71	46	368
Whitelands, Chelsea. (Mistresses.)	2 yrs.	9	16	15	21	17	78
Smith Square Institn. W'minster (Mistresses)	6 mths.	62	92	89	93	75	411
		148	213	230	244	207	1042

[21] See (Ed.) Young: *Early Victorian England*, p. 337: "In a provincial capital," he (Dr. Chalmers) says in his treatise on Voluntary Assistance, "the great mass of the population are retained in kindly and immediate dependence on the wealthy residenters of the place . . . This brings the two extreme orders of society into the sort of relationship which is highly favourable to the general blandness and tranquillity of the whole population. In a manufacturing town, on the other hand, the poor and wealthy stand more disjoined from each other. It is true they often meet, but they meet more in the arena of contest than in a field where the patronage and custom of one party are met by the gratitude and goodwill of the other."

[22] "Letter to J. P. K. Shuttleworth," July, 1846, privately printed, but not published. For Wm. Harness (1790–1869). See the *D.N.B.*

[23] See H. M. Beatty: *Brief History of Education*, 1922, p. 153, note: "In 1841 the Grant for the Royal Stables at Windsor was three times greater than the education grants."

[24] "Remarks on Dr. Hook's Letter," 1846.

[25] See the *D.N.B.*

[26] *Observations on Village School Education, with suggestions for its improvement*, by the Rev. R. A. Gordon. This is highly practical and notable especially for its time-tables.

[27] *Church Schools and State Interference*, p. 18.

[28] Written in 1853. Page 5: "But though Government could no longer, from the inherent vice of its own constitution—a vice every year more and more developed—deal with the Church of England as the one teacher of the People, still it could not but be very desirous to avail itself of the vast machinery ready to its hand in the parochial schools, provided it could so influence and ultimately alter the character of these schools as to suit its own views and purposes: provided only, that is, that it could succeed in converting the parochial school of THE CATHOLIC CHURCH of England into schools of 'Broad Church of Englishmen.'" Denison says that he imputes bad motives to no one: the State must act according to its nature, for Government has no creed, and he thinks the cry of 'civil and religious liberty' is possibly blasphemous. There was much of Hildebrand in Archdeacon Denison.

On the teaching office of the clergy he says ". . . the clergy are directly and solely responsible for all that is taught in the parish schools, for the matter and the manner of it. For the clergy are in virtue of their office ' the dispensers of the Word of God and of His Holy Sacraments,' and it is upon the Word of God and upon His Holy Sacraments that all Christian Education in any true sense of the word must be based."

Denison then speaks of the (Roman) Catholic position: "I am no lover of Roman Catholicism but I will say that I thank the Roman Catholic Bishops with all my heart for the stand which they are making against a principle (i.e. of displacing clerical control of education) which begins with unsettling and ends with destroying, for all whom it may be allowed to pervade and imbue, the Catholic Faith."

[29] *Church Schools and State Interference*, p. 29.

[30] R. L. Archer: *Secondary Education*, p. 202. See *Life and Letters of Wm. John Butler* (1897), pp. 144 ff., for Wantage Schools and p. 156 for others.

[31] *Remarks occasioned by the present Crusade against the Educational Plans of the Committee of Council on Education*, 1850, p. 64. An illustration of the necessity of "charity" was the founding in 1844 of the (undenominational) Ragged School Union.

[32] There may be much truth in this complaint, but by way of contrast the following piece of pastoral advice from a clergyman is nothing less than the application in miniature of the principle of differential payments for the same thing. "The instruction given to the children paying at an advanced rate should in no way differ from that given to the labourer's sons. If it does, a jealousy will arise on the part of the poorer parents, which it will be difficult to allay. Another advantage may arise from this: that harsh separation of one rank in society from another, with all the selfish jealousy it engenders, now prevailing, may hereafter be stopped, and those who twenty or twenty-five years hence will be employers, mechanics, and labourers in our villages, will remember, for their good, the days when they stood side by side in the parish church before their pastor to be catechized, or knelt at the same form in the village school-room for daily prayers." Nat. Soc. Monthly Paper, No. LI, of March, 1851, p. 82. See also Sir John Pakington's evidence in the Schools Inquiry Commission Report, Vol. IV, pp. 674 ff., where the distinctions in a number of parish schools correspond to grades of instruction and not of social class.

[33] *Remarks*, p. 11. On pp. 20–21 he is aggrieved because it is not generally known, although admitted by Archdeacon Sinclair, for many years Treasurer of the National Society, that the Committee of Council's management clause would secure church schools in church hands and prevent Dissenting managers getting a foothold. Yet on June 12th, 1852, the Committee of Council issued a minute to redress the position of the clergy and laity of the Church of England (as compared with that of the Roman Catholics).

[34] *Ibid.*, p. 53.

[35] *Ibid.*, a contemporary in Manchester, the Rev. C. Richson, visited 132 mills and induced many employers to exhibit the following:—

"Notice—In the Appointment of children and Young Persons in this Establishment.

Those young persons are to be preferred who can Read and Write." (*A Sketch of the Causes, which in Manchester induced the abandonment of the Voluntary System in the support of schools and the Introduction of the Manchester and Salford Education Bill*. 1851. p. 36.)

For a list of his works, see the Bibliography to S. E. Maltby: *Manchester and the Movement for National Elementary Education;* and *Essays on Educational Subjects*, 1857, (Ed.) Alfred Hill, (p. 1) Rev. M.

Mitchell: "On the evidence afforded by the Reports of Her Majesty's Inspectors as to the early age at which children are taken from school." (p. 14) Mr. Flint, H.M.I. on the same.

[36] For a study of the vast range of Victorian charitable work, see Lascelles: "Charity," in Young's *Early Victorian England*, and Sampson Low, Jr., *The Charities of London*, new ed., 1867.

E. CONTINUED PROGRESS OF THE NATIONAL SOCIETY AND THE QUESTION OF EDUCATIONAL DESTITUTION

[1] In 1847 in an estimated population of 17,224,218 there were 955,865 daily scholars. In 1837 in an estimated population of 15,084,941 there were 558,180 daily scholars.

[2] Yet one inspector wrote: "Better teachers, better books, ampler furniture have been provided. Clergyman and schoolmaster have acted as the missionaries of education, and yet, in despite of all, where wages are highest and steadiest the school suffers most." Comm. of Council Report, 1855–6, pp. 496–7.

[3] Fifteen years after the Act of 1870 and ten years after Lord Sandon's Act for compulsory attendance we find one of Her Majesty's Inspectors boldly stating that "the school is not yet a recognized institution." *Ibid.*, 1884–5, p. 327. See also *ibid.*, 1897–8 for complaints about the shortness of school life (pp. 201–2) and bad attendance in the countryside (p. 207).

[4] *Ibid.*, 1855–6, pp. 506–7.

[5] *Ibid.*, pp. 507–28.

[6] *Ibid.*, 1856–7, p. 391. See also the Report for 1861–2, p. 75, where replies sent to a clergyman who attempted to open a school are given:

A. From a respectable tenant farmer.

——————— Farm.

" Dr. Revd.

I will give the same as my neighbour's dos towards the, school but I have alarg Famoly of my own to educate and is expensive to do, I am willing for the low class of peopel to learn to read the, Bibal and to right but shall not contribut to anything more than that for anything more than that I consider to be a great injury to them.

I remain yours
Respectful

To the Revd.———.   ———"

B. From the Squire.

" My dear Sir,

You are well aware of my opinion respecting the educating the poor orders, and after stating last year that I should not again contribute, am surprised at your application."

Her Majesty's Inspector adds to his quotation of the above letters: " In spite of the progress we have made, I am afraid that there are still a great many parishes in somewhat the same state as this."

[7] *Ibid.*, 1855–6, pp. 393 ff.

[8] For the difficulties in rural parishes, and the apathy of farmers and others, see Comm. of Council Report, 1855–6, pp. 343–4. On p. 345 we find a schoolmaster complaining that schooling was not valued because it was forced on the people and was too cheap.

[9] For the Rev. Chas. Richson, see *D.N.B.*

[10] Comm. of Council Report, 1854–5, pp. 517–18.

[11] *Ibid.*, pp. 441 ff.

[12] pp. 70–75. See also *Scheme of Secular Education proposed by the National Public Schools' Association compared with the Manchester and Salford Boroughs' Education Bill*, 1851, p. 156.

[13] S. E. Maltby: *Manchester and the Movement for National Elementary Education, 1800–70* (1918). See especially Chap. VII: "Manchester and Salford Committee on Education and the Conflict of Forces from 1851–7."

[14] *Ibid.*, p. 65 : two "model" schools set up at great expense, also an association for teachers in church schools to improve their professional usefulness in various ways.

[15] *Ibid.*, pp. 65–6.

F. The National Society's Great Inquiry of 1846–7

[1] " Results of the Returns to the General Enquiry made by the National Society into the State and Progress of Schools for the Education of the Poor in the Principles of the Established Church during the Years 1846–7 throughout England and Wales." The figures quoted, however, are for England only. (The Bodleian, the British Museum, and the Cambridge University Library do not, according to the replies of their respective Librarians, possess a copy. It may be seen in the Board of Education Library.)

[2] See p. 10 above.

[3] See Statistical Appendix, (a).

[4] See p. 161.

[5] Report of an Inspector at Wigtoft given in the Nat. Soc. Monthly Paper, No. XVII, of June 30th, 1848.

[6] On this point see the correspondence between teachers on their relations with clergy in *ibid.*, No. LXI, of Dec., 1851. The classic condemnation of bad church teaching is C. L. Marson: *Huppim and Muppim and Ard* (3rd Edition, 1917).

[7] The clause in a standard agreement offered to teachers by church school managers whereby the former could be turned out at a week's notice, after undertaking by way of bond (and not as damages) to hand over one hundred pounds if he refused to vacate the premises, was an iniquitous arrangement. See *ibid.*, No. XXII, of Sept. 30th, 1848, p. 30.

G. The Work of the National Society to the eve of the Act of 1870

[1] The Nat. Soc. Monthly Paper, No. XIV, of Jan. 31st, 1848, p. 4, has an Appendix of specimen applications of parishes for aid in building and maintaining schools. There are reports on schools inspected : No. XV, of Feb. 28th, 1848, has statistics of the populations served by schools seeking aid.

[2] Full details, including time-tables, may be seen in the Nat. Soc. Monthly Papers, No. LIX, of Oct., 1851, pp. 339–41 (at Lichfield, Aug. 11th to 30th, for 14 mistresses and 2 masters); also No. LXII, of Jan., 1852, pp. 6–10 (5 weeks' Harvest Meeting at Hereford). For an urban equivalent, see Nat. Soc. Monthly Paper, No. XXXIX, of March, 1850, p. 97 : " Manchester Church Teachers' Institute " teachers' classes.

[3] An incumbent ordered a *History of England* from the Committee of Council's list as " being about our mark in respect of size and price. None of us knew anything of it. When it is worn out I shall take good care that a more satisfactory one is substituted." It was a Roman Catholic work. (Committee of Council Report, 1858–9, p. 71.) The National Society has been criticized for its " heaviness " as a publisher : here is a clerical correspondent to the Monthly Paper (No. LXII, Jan., 1852) recommending every parish to secure a well-selected library of really attractive books. Those for the young should be " not too lesson-like and ' proper,' but playful and suited to children."

[4] Nat. Soc. Annual Report, 1848, p. 45.

[5] Nat. Soc. Annual Report, 1859, p. ix.

[6] See Statistical Appendix (b), and "Summaries of the Returns to the General Inquiry made by the National Society into the State and Progress of Schools for the Education of the Poor in the Principles of the Established Church during the years 1856–7 throughout England and Wales," 1858. It is an octavo pamphlet of about 70 pp., priced at sixpence. For a report on Progress in Education in Church Schools see Report of Committee of Council, 1855–6, pp. 472–86. Details of Prize Schemes, etc., are given here.

[7] See Statistical Appendix (b) for composition of school management committees.

[8] Rev. Chas. Richson: *A Sketch of the Causes, etc.,* p. 50. Also on the attendance of children at schools in, e.g. Hull, St. Stephen's (8/15), Manchester, St. Michael's (3/4); Salford, St. Bartholomew (2/3); see a table for various schools in Report of the Committee of Council, 1845, Vol. II, p. 81, and the same, 1855–6, p. 471:

Length of School Age in Lancashire and Staffs.

	At School 2 years or more.	Pupils above ten years old.
1854.	30 %	27 %
1855.	36 %	32 %

" Where school age has been hitherto deplorably low."

[9] For details of an evening school at the National Society's Central School, Westminster, see Nat. Soc. Monthly Papers, Nos. XXXV, of Nov. 1849, p. 261; XLIX, of Jan. 1851, pp. 49–50; LX, of Nov. 1851, pp. 380–2 for an evening school of 120 members at Bury, Lancs. Also see " Remarks upon Evening Schools," in pp. 120–6 of Comm. of Council Report, 1858–9, for mention of clergy and wives teaching in rural evening schools. In the 1855–6 Report of the Comm. of Council are particulars of progress in education through night schools (pp. 483–5).

[10] For details of efficient schools at Crofts, Yorks, supplemented by facts illustrating the manner and extent in which the children's education bettered their condition in life, see Appendix C, p. 309 of the 1857 Committee of Council's Report.

[11] Nat. Soc. Annual Report, 1858, pp. xi. ff. It is added that " The increase will be found in the forthcoming summaries," but only under diocesan headings and not in summaries for England are these given.

[12] See Nat. Soc. Monthly Paper, LXII, of Jan., 1852, p. 14, on the after care of elementary school children: teach them sound doctrine, have faith and fear not. Obliterate all trace of class distinctions, e.g. a choir distinctive in surplices also hides differences in clothes concealed. Also for after care of pauper Industrial School children at Norwood by the Rev. J. Brown and annual re-union of old pupils, see Report of Committee of Council, 1841–2, pp. 389–90.

[13] Comm. of Council Report, 1856–7, pp. 313–14, Appendix C.

[14] *Ibid.,* Appendix D.

[15] *Ibid.,* Appendix F.

[16] *Ibid.,* 1863–4, pp. 121–5.

[17] *Ibid.,* 1861–2, p. 85.

[18] *Ibid.,* 1859–60, p. 89.

[19] Nat. Soc. Annual Report, 1860, p. viii.

[20] *Ibid.,* p. xxxiii.

[21] *Ibid.,* p. ix.

[22] See Appendices VII and VIII, p. xxxiii. ff., in *ibid.,* 1861.

[23] *Ibid.,* 1865, p. xlviii.

[24] p. xi.

[25] *Ibid.,* 1867, p. 17.

[26] See Statistical Appendix (d).

K

[27] See Note 8, p. 128. The National Society first made grants to "Ambulatory Teachers" as such in 1866 (£150), and in 1867 gave £245, in 1868 £220, but these sums soon declined with the number of such teachers.

[28] p. 47, Appendix XII.

[29] For a clerical condemnation see Rev. T. R. Birks: *The Revised Code, What would it do? What should be done with it?* 1862, also Sir Jas. Kay-Shuttleworth: *Memorandum on Popular Education,* 1868. Many clerical writers (e.g. F. J. A. Hort) saw the evil results the Code promised and attacked it in print.

[30] Nat. Soc. Annual Report, 1869, Appendix XVII, p. 78.

[31] *Ibid.,* pp. 29 ff. We may note the Committee of Council in the Report for 1856–7 (p. 270) complaining of the paucity of schools for farmers and tradesmen ("the £10 householder class"): twenty years later (Report of 1876–7, p. 421) they were doing the same of the need for higher class elementary schools for well-to-do mechanics.

[32] See the figures given in Parliament in 1870 by Lord Robt. Montagu (National Education Union Verbatim Report, pp. 20, col. 2 ff.) and Earl de Grey and Ripon (*ibid.,* pp. 516, col. 2 ff.).

[33] "Report of Committee on Primary National Education, Feb. 11th, 1870": pp. 3–10, deal with Educational Destitution. See also a report by a distinguished clerical educationist, the Rev. Wm. Gover. "Day School Education in the Borough of Birmingham: our progress, position, and needs," 1867.

[34] "My lords, it seems to be generally supposed that the extent of education is to be measured by the Returns of the Privy Council. But the only schools which appear on the books of the Privy Council, and consequently only those which appear in their Returns, are schools which receive Government aid in some form or other. But beyond these there is a large number of schools of which, for various reasons, the Privy Council takes no cognizance." (The Bishop of London in the House of Lords, March 8th, 1869. Hansard, Third Series, Vol. CXCIV, p. 822, col. 1.)

[35] Mr. W. E. Forster in introducing his Bill in 1870. (National Education Union. Verbatim Report, p. 6.)

H. Pioneer Village Schools and Similar Efforts

[1] Accounts of the King's Somborne Schools are many: see especially Rd. Dawes: *Schools and other Similar Institutions for the Industrial Classes,* 1853; *An Account of the King's Somborne School,"* n.d.; *Hints on an Improved and Self-Paying System of National Education suggested from the working of the Village School of King's Somborne, in Hampshire,* 4th Edn. n.d.

[2] Committee of Council Report, 1847–8, Vol. I, pp. 16 ff. Appendix on King's Somborne School by the Rev. Hy. Moseley.

[3] Richd. Dawes: *Hints,* p. 4.

[4] Rev. Hy. Moseley's Appendix, p. 19.

[5] *Ibid.,* pp. 23 ff.

[6] *Ibid.* See Young: *Early Victorian England,* p. 342, for the appalling state of "endowed" elementary schools. They represent the measure of national indifference.

[7] *School Payments.*   *Books Bought by Pupils at Cost (to nearest £).*

School Payments.			Books Bought by Pupils at Cost (to nearest £).
1st Year	£57.		£7.
2nd	„	69.	8.
3rd	„	84.	11.
4th	„	93.	15.
5th	„	145.	25.
6th	„	146.	30.
7th	„	165.	39.

[8] Dawes: *Hints,* pp. 8–9. But the Rev. Henry Moseley's Appendix gives the following facts: Boys' School (Master and Assistant), Girls' (Mistress), Infants' (Mistress), and *six* (not four) pupil teachers. There were *two* dames' schools.

[9] p. 23, see also *ibid.,* 1845, Vol. II, p. 33: of incumbents in general— "Whilst the clergyman founds upon the labours of the school his hopes for a *future* (italics quoted) generation, he thus finds them, under the blessing of God, not without fruit in the present."

[10] Report of the Committee of Council, 1841–2, pp. 103–4.

[11] *Ibid.,* p. 102.

[12] Dawes: *Hints,* p. 8.

[13] *Ibid.,* pp. 16 ff.

[14] See also Schools Inquiry Commission, Vol. IV, pp. 698 ff. Schools of this kind in fact were really "Higher Grade" schools.

[15] pp. 240–1. See also an anonymous pamphlet: "A Short Account of the St. Thomas's, Charterhouse, Schools." (It is the work of the Rev. W. Rogers, according to the Nat. Soc. Monthly Paper, No. LXII, of Jan., 1852, pp. 5–6.) Also see the second Report of the Cross Commission, pp. 94 ff. Rogers also produced accounts in 1854, 1856, 1857, also "Educational Prospects of St. Thomas, Charterhouse," 1854.

[16] Report of the Comm. of Council, 1857–8, pp. 243–4.

[17] For Wm. ("Hang Theology") Rogers (1819–96), see the *D.N.B.,* also his racy and diverting *Reminiscences* (1888). He was one of the Newcastle Commissioners. Pp. 48 ff. deal with St. Thomas, Charterhouse. See p. 90: "The eastern portion of the district was made over to Mr. Main Walrond, the present Vicar of St. Lawrence Jewry. He came to it in all the ardour and freshness of youth, and for nine years stuck to it like a man. Then he fled. He had gone the pace as hard as I had. Golden Lane cost him £5,000."

[18] DAY SCHOOLS.

    Boys. I. *Upper School for Sons of Tradesmen.*
                  80 Boys. Fees £1 per quarter, or 15/-.

          II. *National School.*
                  260 Boys. Fees 3d., 4d., 6d. per week.

        III. *Free School for Boys.*
                  90 Boys.   *Total,* 430 Boys.

    Girls. 160 *Girls.* Fees 3d. to 1/- per week.

    Infants. I. *1st Division.* 70 Boys and Girls. Fees 4d. per week.
                2nd Division. 200 Girls. *Total,* 430 Girls and Infants.

    Classes. 30 pupils learn French and pay 2/6 per month.
             80 pupils learn drawing under a master from S. Kensington and pay 2/- per month.

The cost of the schools was £1,000, but fees brought in only £700

[19] *Work—the law of God and lot of Man,* 1852, pp. 24–36.

[20] See two anonymous pamphlets—"On Self-Supporting Schools of Industry or Mental Discipline, 1844" (p. 36) and "Poor Rates Reduced by Self-Supporting Reading, Writing and Agricultural Schools. Dedicated to Bp. Gilbert of Chichester, 1844" (p. 12), also G. C. T. Bartley: *Schools for the People* (1871), pp. 243–55.

[21] Committee of Council Report, 1856–7, p. 315, Appendix E; for the girls' work, see *ibid.,* 1866–7, pp. 168–9.

[22] *Ibid.,* pp. 474–6.

[23] *Ibid.,* 1841–2, pp. 174 ff; and 1843, pp. 539 ff.

[24] For W. L. Rham, see the *D.N.B.,* also Report of Committee of Council, 1843, pp. 545 ff.

[25] See *Essays on Educational Subjects Read at the Educational Conference of June, 1857.* Ed. by Alfred Hill. (1857.) p. 279. Yorke later became dean of Worcester.

[26] See the Comm. of Council Report, 1846, pp. 535 and 539 respectively for the appalling list of ailments of pupils at the Manchester and Liverpool Schools of Industry.

[27] *Ibid.,* pp. 266 ff.

[28] *Official Year Book of the Church of England,* 1937, p. 508.

[29] Personal information.

[30] *Official Year Book of the Church of England,* 1937, p. 508.

[31] Report of Committee of Council, 1855–6, pp. 472–86.

[32] "The Hans Town School of Industry" was established as early as 1804: it trained girls in churchmanship, the three Rs and domestic science duties.

[33] Report of the Committee of Council, 1861–2, pp. 76–78. Also *ibid.,* 1875–6, p. 354 for the cookery school at Walton, where the food was carried by the pupils to the sick and aged of the parish.

[34] Committee of Council Report, 1857–8, pp. 420–6.

[35] *Ibid.,* 1860–1, pp. 105–6.

[36] *Ibid.,* 1861–2, p. 91.

[37] *Ibid.,* p. 91.

[38] The Nat. Soc. Monthly Paper, No. CLXVII, of Oct., 1860, p. 295, has an attack by a working man on these "ragged schools" as a social danger: the better sort are driving out the poorest boys, who really belong there, from the parish schools.

[39] The Newcastle Report has some trenchant remarks by Mr. Herbert Birley (who, on the testimony of an H.M.I., knew more about Manchester education than any man living and whose family have similarly led the city's education in our day) on the Committee of Council's refusal to help St. Phillip's on the grounds of "red tape" (Vol. V, p. 108).

[40] Report of the Committee of Council, 1861–2, pp. 71–2.

[41] See Nat. Soc. Monthly Paper, No. LVI, of July, 1851. For their hard lot see also *ibid.,* No. CXXX, of Sept., 1857, p. 266.

[42] *Ibid.,* No. LIX, of Oct., 1851, pp. 350–1.

[43] p. 468.

[44] *Memorials of St. Mark's College,* Ed. by the Rev. G. W. Gent, M.A. (1891): article by A. C. King, quoting the Rev. George Atkins, pp. 57–58.

[45] Report of Committee of Council, 1886–7, p. 313.

[46] *Ibid.,* 1890–1, p. 387, and 1891–2, p. 88.

[47] See his "A Letter to Mr. Senior on Supplemental Evening Schools" (1839) and Newcastle Report (1861), Vol. I, pp. 39 ff.

[48] Maurice: *Life of F. D. Maurice,* Vol. I, p. 482.

[49] He quotes W. J. Fox (who had introduced a bill on education in this year) with his solution to the religious problem: "secular instruction with no religious peculiarities and a present to each child on leaving school, of which the scriptures shall form a part!" This is the masterly solution to the "religious difficulty" by a unitarian whose "tolerance" cost him nothing.

[50] Report, Vol. V, pp. 160 ff.

[51] Ollard and Cross: *The Anglo-Catholic Revival in Outline,* p. 63.

[52] See Eleanor F. Rawnsley: *Canon Rawnsley* (1923), esp. pp. 155–65.

[53] Committee of Council Report, 1852–3, p. 244.

[54] *Ibid.,* 1855–6, p. 402.

[55] *Ibid.,* 1858–9, pp. 70–1; also 1855–6, pp. 472–86.

[56] *Ibid.,* 1870–1, p. 223.

[57] S. Baring-Gould: *Hawker of Morwenstow,* p. 226.

[58] Report of the Committee of Council, 1872–3, p. 182.

[59] *Ibid.,* p. 195.

[60] See *Essays on Educational Subjects read at the Educational Conference,* 1857, pp. 346 ff.

I. THE NEW ERA: 1870–1914

[1] New and revised edition, 1929, Vol. II, pp. 461–2. For the exchange of views in the debate the obvious reference is to Hansard, but much more convenient is a single volume: *National Education Union. A verbatim report, with indices of the Debate in Parliament during the Progress of the Elementary Education Bill, 1870, together with a reprint of the Act.*

[2] Report of the Committee of Council, 1870–1, pp. 117–28, has a survey of the period 1847–70 by the Rev. M. Mitchell, who was an H.M.I. during those years. He pays special tribute to his colleague, Canon Moseley, and the late bishop of Bath and Wells, i.e. R. J. Eden, 3rd baron Auckland (1799–1870): see his *Charges* of 1855, 1858, 1861. See also in the *D.N.B.*, Sir J. S. Pakington (1799–1880), a churchman, progressive and tolerant, who introduced various bills on education. See T. Raymont: *A History of the Education of Young Children* (1937), for a tribute to the Rev. M. Mitchell's pioneer work, as an H.M.I., for infant schools.

[3] See the Report of the Committee of Council, 1875–6, p. 367, where the vicar of St. Jude's, Bristol, and the master of a Board school are both quoted to show that parents are in the habit of sending their children for the minimum number of attendances required by law and thus upset the school organization.

[4] See *Memorials of St. Mark's College,"* (Ed.) Rev. G. W. Gent, 1891, p. 14. "It is said that Mr. Lowe, when it was suggested to him that his proposed legislation would destroy the Training Colleges, replied: ' Do you suppose I shall regret that? ' Genuine or not, these words accurately reflect the attitude of his Code towards the teachers."

[5] *Ibid.*, p. 24.

[6] *Ibid.*, p. 25.

[7] *Voluntary Schools and State Education."* An archidiaconal charge, 1894, p. 13 ; see also *James M. Wilson, 1836–1931*—an autobiography edited and published after his death.

[8] Even competition: the Vicar of Child's Wickham built a school and teacher's house on the glebe costing £525. The land-owner, not a churchman, set up a rival school. (Report of Committee of Council, 1866–7, pp. 40–1.)

[9] Nat. Soc. Annual Report, 1871, p. 10.

[10] *Ibid.*, p. 11. Local effort naturally continued: e.g. " In Halsall the additions to the National School recommended by the Department have been made by the rector of the parish at his own cost." (Comm. of Council Report, 1876–7, p. 445.)

[11] *Ibid.*, 1872, p. 9.

[12] *Ibid.*, 1873, p. 11. There is here a table of annual income for the years 1856–72, i.e. from the Cessation of the Queen's Letter income to the Act of 1870. Legacies in the 1873 Report (p. 12), amount to £6,338.

[13] *Ibid.*, p. 14. Bishop Otter College was described in the Report of the Committee of Council, 1877–8, p. 435 : " No institution in England is more deserving of public support or patronage."

[14] Report of Committee of Council, 1870–1, p. 91.

[15] *Ibid.*, p. 200.

[16] *Ibid.*, p. 201.

[17] *Ibid.*, p. 220.

[18] *Ibid.*, 1872–3, pp. 50–51.

[19] Nat. Soc. Annual Report, 1874, p. 10.

[20] *Ibid.*, Appendix XXI, p. 63.

[21] p. 7.

[22] *Ibid.*, p. 8. By August 1874 the position was as follows:

Scholars in Elementary Schools.

Church of England Schools	1,117,461.
British, Wesleyan and other Nonconformist Schools	322,633.
Roman Catholic Schools	100,372.
Board Schools	138,293.
Total	1,678,759.

[23] Yet see the Report of the Committee of Council, 1871–2, pp. 48–9: "There will be few school boards in Gloucestershire so long as their initiation is left to the free action of the inhabitants."

[24] Nat. Soc. Annual Report, 1875, p. 12.

[25] See Statistical Appendix (e) I. The figures are from Nat. Soc. Annual Report, 1876, p. 8. From the Returns of the Education Department. See "Return, showing by Counties, for each Public Elementary School in England and Wales, the average number of scholars in attendance, amount of Government grant for annual maintenance, the number of children for whom accommodation was provided and the Statement of income and expenditure. For the year ending 31st Aug., 1876, (1877)."

[26] *Ibid.*, 1877, p. 13.

[27] *Ibid.*, p. 61. Appendix XVII.

[28] *Ibid.*, 1878, p. 10.

[29] This was subsequently taken by the S.P.C.K. into its own hands (the National Society giving £2,000): for its history as St. Katherine's College see Allen and McClure: *Two Hundred Years*, pp. 162 and 164.

[30] Nat. Soc. Annual Report, 1878, p. 13. For some notes on the "City of London Auxiliary School Association," founded by Joshua Watson and friends in 1812, see the Report of the Committee of Council, 1879–80, pp. 376–8: "pioneers of a system which has now overwhelmed them in its development." Buildings were erected, £1,200 annually provided for maintenance and there were 750–1,160 children under instruction each year.

[31] Nat. Soc. Annual Report, 1879, pp. 11–12.

[32] pp. 8 ff. See Statistical Appendix, (e) 2.

[33] Nat. Soc. Annual Report, 1881, pp. 9–10. Here is an H.M.I's verdict: "To the promoters of voluntary schools it may with justice be said that their continued prosperity through the crisis of 1870 and their present success is their complete justification and their great encouragement." Committee of Council Report, 1876–7, p. 507.

[34] Report of the Committee of Council, 1877–8, p. 419.

[35] *Ibid.*, 1875–6, p. xxv. Details of school board expenditure immediately precedes this. For possible evils in country school boards—which were not uncommon—see Comm. of Council Report, 1876–7, pp. 571–2. There is also a contrast between the Voluntary and school board systems. In the Report of 1876–7, p. 543, is a table showing the importance of good management—Church schools come first and Board schools last. A report we cannot pass over is *ibid.*, 1894–5, pp. 4–6, on the slackness of country school boards (p. 6): "Thus, here and there, do 'the rude fore-fathers of the hamlet' nip the budding intellect of ingenuous youth, and repress the 'noble rage' of the teacher! What a penny-wise, pound-foolish system!"

[36] Report of the Committee of Council, 1876–7, p. 435. See also p. 527 for the Bishop of Carlisle's speech to his own Diocesan Conference on the *positive* side of school boards.

[37] Nat. Soc. Annual Report, 1881, p. 10.

[38] *Ibid.*, p. 17.

[39] Nat. Soc. Annual Report, 1881, p. 20.

[40] Nat. Soc. Annual Report, 1881, p. 20.

[41] The Voluntary Schools Act, 1897, exempted Voluntary Schools " from the Rates."

[42] *Ibid.*, p. 22.

[43] p. 10.   See Statistical Appendix, (e) 3.

[44] For a peroration of Mr. Gladstone on the aims and principles of the National Society see Nat. Soc. Monthly Paper VI of 6th June, 1847, pp. 4–8.

[45] Nat. Soc. Annual Report, 1884, p. 31.

[46] p. 9.   The Cross Commission, 1st Report, 1886, p. 519, gives the following figures for elementary schools:

Year.	Endowments.	Voluntary Subscriptions.	School pence.	Other sources.	Cost of Maintenance.
1885.	£134,614.	£583,936.	£872,502.	£31,708.	£2,935,463.

State Grant £1,350,098.

The evidence of the Secretary of the National Society since 1870, the Rev. J. Duncan, occupies pp. 396–433.

[47] pp. 9 ff.   See Statistical Appendix, (e) 4.

[48] p. 21.   Two illustrations of students at work in the National Society's Cookery School are to be seen in Bott and Clephane: *Our Mothers*, p. 61. (1932.)

[49] For pioneer work in cookery in schools see Nat. Soc. Annual Report, 1898, pp. 34–42.   Appendices II and III.

[50] p. 42.   See also " Summary of the Replies to the National Society Enquiry as to the Condition and Prospects of Church Schools in School Board Districts." (1893.)

[51] Nat. Soc. Annual Report, 1897, p. 25.   He quotes the Education Department, Feb., 1895, on " Religious Teaching in Board Schools."

In which neither Bible read, nor oral instruction given	7
In which the Bible read, without note or comment	75
In which no definite syllabus, but instruction left to the teacher's discretion	52
In which there is definite syllabus and real teaching	101
	235

[52] See Chapter VII (pp. 103 ff.) of W. Foxley Norris: *Elementary Schools*, 1904.   (Handbooks for the Clergy.)   The Act of 1891 recognized the principle of Voluntary Associations (Fee Grant); the 1897 Voluntary Schools Act dealt with the " Aid Grant."

[53] Report of Committee of Council, 1894–5, p. 77, by W. P. Turnbull, H.M.I.

[54] *Ibid.*, p. 3.

[55] p. 14.

[56] Nat. Soc. Annual Report, 1901, p. 27. See Statistical Appendix, (e) 5.

[57] See Statistical Appendix, (e) VI.

[58] Nat. Soc. Annual Report, 1903, pp. 9 ff.

[59] *Ibid.*, 1904, p. 29.

[60] *Ibid.*, 1914, p. 10.

[61] See Statistical Appendix, (e) VII.

[62] Nat. Soc. Annual Report, 1913, p. 19.

[63] *Ibid.*, p. 36.

[64] *Ibid.*, p. 35.

[65] *Ibid.*, 1913, p. 18.

[66] *Ibid.*, pp. 23–24.

[67] See pp. 9 ff. of the 1939 Annual Report.

[68] See Statistical Appendix, (e) VIII.

[60] pp. 28–30 of the 1939 Report. In 1907 Miss Hetty Lee's important work *New Methods in the Junior Sunday School* was published, and about that time she became the first organizer for religious teaching of the National Society. The Society has always included Sunday religious teaching in its scope and much good work was done by Miss Lee to improve Sunday School work throughout the country.

[70] Bell: *Randall Davidson*, Vol. II, pp. 899 ff.

[71] See the Report of the Unofficial Conference between certain members of the Anglican and Free Churches (Appendix IV) below, which met in 1937 and reported in 1938. Co-operation with the Institute of Christian Education (founded 1936, under Canon Tissington Tatlow, inter-denominational) is part of the same policy.

J. THE WORK OF OTHER CENTRAL BODIES

[1] See *A Genealogical Account of the Mayo and Elton Families*, by Canon C. H. Mayo, 2nd Edn. 1908. For Chas. Mayo (1792–1846) see pp. 265–71 and Elizabeth Mayo (1793–1865) pp. 279–82. James Mayo of Wimborne (1784–1851) showed great zeal for national schools. T. Raymont: *History of the Education of Young Children*, has sympathetic references, and places the society in the evolution of the technique of infant teaching.

[2] E. C. Tufnell's report of the Home and Colonial School Society in Committee of Council Report, 1846, p. 544; pp. 555–6 include a Table of Receipts and Expenditure.

[3] *Ibid.*, pp. 544 ff. The Newcastle Commission Report (Vol. I, p. 575) has the following table:

Society.	Expended in 1859.	Expended since Foundation.
Home and Colonial	£8,776	£116,000
Church Education	£2,761	£10,071
National	£15,811	£724,599
British and Foreign	£15,948	£156,664*

(* In the last ten years only.) The Cross Commission (1st Report, Vol. I, pp. 461 ff.), reported that 130 of the 140 students—for it was now a ladies' college—were churchwomen and altogether 4,500 students had been trained at the college. The Annual Report for 1889–1900 shows its activities as below:

(A) Gray's Inn Road Training College for Women Teachers, includes Kindergarten Department (state aided).

(B) Department for Women Teachers in Secondary Schools, Highbury Hill House, N. (non-state aided).

(C) Model and Practising Schools.

    (i) Infants under 7 (250, each paying 4d. per week).
    (ii) Junior Mixed School (each pupil pays 4d.–9d. p.w.).
    (iii) Reynolds Higher Grade School (150 girls, each paying 9d. —1/- p.w.).

[4] Proceeds from capital were (to the nearest £) £19; from annual subscriptions £82; donations £11; legacy £50; grant from the National Society £154; and the rest came from grants for students in training.

[5] pp. 9 ff.

[6] See "Report of the Proceedings at the Opening of the New Home and Colonial College, Wood Green" (1904).

[7] p. 11.

[8] *Official Year Book of the Church of England*, 1937, p. 638.

[9] *Official Year Book of the Church of England*, 1937, p. 638.

[10] *Ibid.*, p. 494.

[11] *Ibid.*, p. 636.

[12] For what is claimed as the first ragged boys' picnic and excursion, see Maurice: *Life of F. D. Maurice*, Vol. I, p. 548.

[13] G. C. Binyon: *Christian Socialist Movement in England* (1931) D. O. Wagner: *Church of England and Social Reform since 1834* (Columbia Univ. Press, 1930).

[14] See Maurice B. Reckitt: *Faith and Society* (1932) and references therein. G. L. Prestige: *Life of Charles Gore* must be mentioned. The Bishop of Chichester's (G. K. A. Bell) *Randall Davidson*, will be a revelation to many of what the great Primate's work for church and state really amounted to.

[15] It is interesting to compare the mind of the Oxford Conference on Church Community and State of 1938 (Vol. VI on Education) with anything that the Board of Education can produce (e.g. Spens Report, 1938, pp. 206 ff.) to see the urgent need of the element that Christian thought *per se* alone can produce.

[16] S. C. Carpenter: *Church and People*, p. 330.

[17] 1937 edn., pp. 509 ff., for youth movement and Sunday School work, pp. 516 ff. for higher religious education.

[18] See *The Working Men's College (1854–1904)* by J. Llewellyn Davies; *Working Men's Clubs and Educational Institutes* (1867, 2nd Edn. 1904); also *Spiritual Values in Adult Education*, 2 Vols. (1925) by Basil A. Yeaxlee, which has valuable material. For the Bible Classes at Queen's Square, that led to the College, see Maurice, *Life of F. D. Maurice*, Vol. I, pp. 488 ff., also the Schools Inquiry Commn. Report, Vol. X, p. 293, and Vol. VII, pp. 567 ff.

K. THE CHURCH'S TRAINING COLLEGES

[1] See " Report from the Select Committee on Education of the Poorer Classes," 1838, pp. 78 ff., for the Rev. J. C. Wigram on the central and modern schools at Westminster. There were also 46 other training schools —of little value.

[2] See Prof. Frank Smith: *Life of Sir James Kay-Shuttleworth*.

[3] *Four Periods of Public Education*, 1862, Second Period, pp. 294–375.

[4] Vol. II, pp. 7–78.

[5] See above pp. 14–15 and p. 24.

[6] A conspectus of the provision for teachers' training is in Comm. of Council Report, 1845, Vol. I, pp. 333–4. Pp. 334–389 deal with St. Mark's College and Chester Training College, but include much other valuable material.

Institution.	Number in Training.	Period of Training.
St. Mark's College.	53	3 years
Battersea.	71	1½ years +
Whitelands.	54	2 years +
Westminster (Manchester Buildings).	40	6 mos. to 1 year
Westminster (Smith Square).	51	do.
Canterbury.	5 men 4 women	6 mos. +
York and Ripon.	36 men 8 women	1 year + (Exhibitioners 3 yrs.)
Durham.	13	—
Winchester.	19	6 mos. +
Chichester.	10 (13 before Xmas)	2 years
Brighton.	11	1 year
Exeter.	19	3 years

Institution.	Number in Training.	Period of Training.
Bristol.	6	3 years
Lichfield.	26	2 years
Lincoln.	(The school, which is for the middle classes with a training dept. attached, will accommodate 60 boarders)	—
Llandaff.	2 men 2 women	3–12 mos.
Norwich.	Day Training Establishment	—
Oxford.	14 men	1 year +
Kidlington.*	av. 10	6 mos. +
Salisbury.	26	6 mos. — 3 years
Chester.	41	1 year
Warrington.	20	—

(At Chester and Lincoln there were middle class schools and at Smith's Square a Girls' Infant School for the Middle Classes.)

* " . . . belonging to the amalgamated Diocese of Gloucester and Oxford." *(Three Oxfordshire Parishes,* p. 168, being Vol. XXIV, 1893, pub. by the Oxford Hist. Society.) It removed to Fishponds about 1849. ("Further Additions and Corrections," p. 2, to above.)

[7] *Memorials of St. Mark's College,* Ed. by Rev. G. W. Gent, M.A. (1891), p. 36. From 1841–8 the College was run by a sub-committee of the National Society, but since 1848 it has had its own council. See also Nat. Soc. Annual Report, 1905, pp. 18–22, for a historical note on the College. The Cross Commission, 1st Report, Vol. I, pp. 468 ff. has the evidence of the Principal of St. Mark's; pp. 493 ff. of the Lady Principal of Bp. Otter College. See also the same Commission's " Training College Returns of Information " requested by circular.

[8] *Ibid.,* p. 5.

[9] See M. Graham Brown: *Training in Truro—1813–38;* G. Ashley Wood: *History of Hockerill Training College;* Thomas Adkins: *History of St. John's College, Battersea;* pp. 175 ff. may show a generation that has forgotten what sort of man Canon Evan Daniel was. He began as a pupil and became principal and a well-known writer.

[10] " Training College Commission Report to the Abp. of Canterbury, Nov., 1916," p. 6.

[11] pp. 643 ff. of Vol. I, also see Vol. IV, pp. 391 ff. (As Colleges have changed their name or site or been amalgamated or closed down, their present name or position has been added to make identification clear. These details are taken as given in the Report, but the Church's 1933 Committee of Inquiry Report quoted below offers minor differences.

Men.	Training College.	Date of Foundation.	Av. No. of Students.
	Chester (Ch.)	1839	53
Bp. Otter:	Chichester (Ch.)	,,	17
Women's College after 1872.			
	Lichfield (Ch.)	,, (closed)	Not inspected
	Exeter (Ch.)	,,	44
	Winchester (Ch.)	,,	37
St. Mark &	Battersea (Ch.)	1840	109
St. John, Chelsea.	St. Mark's (Ch.)	1841	105
(Bede.)	Durham (Ch.)	1841	47
	Carnarvon (Ch.)	1846	36
Now separate.	York & Ripon (Ch.)	,,	Not inspected
	Carmarthen (Ch.)	1848	36

Men.	Training College.	Date of Foundation	Av. No. of Students.
Highbury College.	Metropolitan (Ch.)	1849 (Closed as a Ch. College, 1909)	72
(Birmingham.)	Saltley (Ch.)	1852	59
	Hammersmith (R.C.)	„	46
	Culham (Ch.)	1853	56
	Bangor (Br.)	—	20
	Peterborough (Ch.)	1857 (Closed 1938)	15
Women.	Gray's Inn Road (Ch.)	1836 (To Wood Green 1903. Closed 1928)	172
	Salisbury (Ch.)	1840	60
	Norwich (Ch.)	1840	39
(Putney.)	Whitelands (Ch.)	1841	106
	Brighton (Ch.)	1842 (Closed 1938)	45
(Transferred to Liverpool, 1930)	Warrington (Ch.)	1844	90
	York & Ripon (Ch.)	1846	109
	Truro (Ch.)	1849 (Closed 1938)	21
	Derby (Ch.)	1851	40
(Hockerill.)	Bishop's Stortford (Ch.)	1852	57
(Fishponds, Bristol.)	Bristol, Gloucester and Oxford (Ch.)	1853	69
(St. Hild's.)	Durham (Ch.)	1858	37
	Liverpool (R.C.)	—	51
	St. Leonards (R.C.)	—	31
Mixed.	Borough Road (Br.)	—	130
(St. Paul's, Men.)	Cheltenham (Ch.)	1848	155
(St. Mary's, Women.)	Westminster (Wesleyan)	—	102
	Homerton (Congregational)	—	Not inspected

York and Ripon early split up: the York college training men and the Ripon college women. There is no need to stress the preponderance of the Church's effort, or her initiative, for they are strikingly clear in the table above.

(Ch. — Church.

Br. — British of Undenominational.)

R.C. — Roman Catholic.

The cost of building, enlarging and improving colleges was as follows (the Govt. grant included being shown in brackets):

13   men's colleges (Ch. inspected only) £162,000 (£49,000) approx.
13   women's colleges („   „   „) £87,000 (£31,000)   „

In 1859 the total income of 15 inspected Church colleges for Schoolmasters was as follows (the Govt. grant included being shown in brackets and expressed as a percentage):

Approx. £42,000 (£32,000 — 76·0%)

The corresponding figures for the women's 13 colleges were:
Approx. £38,000 (£29,000 — 73·9%)

[12] Derwent Coleridge: *Education of the People*, p. 5.
[13] p. 44.
[14] pp. 58 ff.

[15] *Report of Committee of Enquiry, 1933,* p. 70.

MEN.		WOMEN.	
Birmingham	180	Bishop's Stortford	160
Cheltenham	180	Brighton	160
Chelsea	200	Bristol	150
Chester	160	Cheltenham	200
Culham	90	Chichester	150
Durham	180	Derby	165
Exeter	180	Durham	150
Winchester	160	Kennington	190
York	200	Lincoln	160
		Norwich	134
		Peterborough	150
		Putney	220
		Ripon	139
		Salisbury	180
		Tottenham	160
		Truro	150
		Warrington	200

The Totals are 4,348 students.

[16] See F. J. C. Hearnshaw: *Centenary History of King's College, London: 1828–1929* (1929).

[17] C. E. Whiting: *University of Durham, 1832–1932* (1932), and J. T. Fowler: *Durham University* (1904) in the " College Histories " Series.

L. PARLIAMENTARY TRIBUTES TO THE CHURCH'S WORK

(References are to Hansard, save where indication is to the contrary.)

[1] Third Series. Vol. CI, p. 262, col. 1.
[2] Third Series. Vol. CXCIV, p. 807, col. 1
[3] National Education Union, Verbatim Report, p. 6, col. 2.
[4] See also *ibid.,* p. 51, col. 1.
[5] *Ibid.,* p. 81, col. 1.
[6] Third Series. Vol. CLXVI, p. 86, col. 2.
[7] *Ibid.,* p. 90, col. 2.
[8] *Ibid.,* p. 95, cols. 1 and 2.
[9] See also the speech of Mr. Whiteside, *ibid.,* March 27th, pp. 138, col. 1 ff.
[10] National Education Union, Verbatim Report, p. 21, col. 1.
[11] Third Series. Vol. CLXXXV, 1158.
[12] *Ibid.,* 1162.
[13] National Education Union, Verbatim Report, p. 8, col. 1. ·
[14] *Ibid.,* p. 19, col. 1.
[15] *Ibid.,* p. 19, col. 2.
[16] *Ibid.,* p. 176, col. 1.
[17] See also Mr. Gladstone's speech, pp. 280, col. 1 ff.

II. THE CHURCH'S CONTRIBUTION TO SECONDARY EDUCATION

[1] This chapter presented unusual difficulties, and perhaps our best comment may be taken from Lowndes: *Silent Social Revolution,* p. 45.

" To the modern investigator of the educational system of 40 years ago no feature presents more baffling problems than the extent of the provision for education above the elementary stage. Despite the 9 volumes of the Report of the Royal Commission on Secondary Education and the annual output of the Charity Commission, the Science and Art Department, the figures either do not exist at all or have to be extracted from lists of schools running into many hundreds of pages. Moreover, no attempt ever appears to have been made either in the Board of Education or elsewhere to clarify the position. The only existing evidence of such an attempt is contained in a Chapter (§ 20, p. 7, and § 24, p. 9) in the Board's Annual Report for 1911–12. This hazards a guess that there were probably about 800 schools, endowed and proprietory, which ultimately became recognized secondary schools."

[2] See Report of the Public Schools Commission (Clarendon), 1861–4.

[3] E.g. Giggleswick and Sedbergh. The Royal Commission on Secondary Education, Vol. VII, pp. 249–51 condemns this tendency.

[4] E.g. between 1843 and 1863 there arose the following—Cheltenham, Marlborough, Rossall, Radley, Wellington, Epsom, Bradfield, Haileybury, Clifton, Malvern: of the day schools we may note Liverpool College, Liverpool Institute, King's College School, University College School, City of London School.

[5] Report of the Committee of Council, 1870–1, pp. 189–90.

[6] See p. 21.

[7] *The Official Year Book of the Church of England,* 1937, pp. 502 ff. has details of the work of the Cathedral Schools.

[8] See K. E. Kirk (Bishop of Oxford): *The Story of the Woodard Schools,* p. 11. Also Sir John Otter: *Life of Nathaniel Woodard.* By Woodard himself, *A plan for the Middle Classes* (1848), and *Letter to Lord Salisbury* (1868), giving respectively the problem and its solution. Also Schools Inquiry Commission, Vol. V, pp. 45 ff. and 71 ff. (for Lancing) and Vol. VII, pp. 135 ff. for the three grades of schools (Lancing, Hurst, Ardingly) for the three classes catered for.

[9] Kirk, *op. cit.,* p. 47.

[10] See *Ibid.,* p. 91, for Woodard's curious educational ladder. And see the Committee of Council Report, 1876–7, p. 511: "When we find Oxford first-class men leaving high positions in our old public-schools in order to train the sons of shopkeepers and farmers at Ardingly and Hurstpierpoint, we may justly feel that this branch of teaching is in the soundest state, a state in which a demand on the part of poor parents willing to make real efforts to secure a thorough training for their children is met by a spirit not of Quixotic, but of reasonable and persistent benevolence on the part of those best qualified to train them."

[11] Kirk, *op. cit.,* pp. 121–2.

[12] *Ibid.,* p. 126.

[13] From the latest edition of the *Church of England Official Year Book* to give statistics (1937), pp. 505 ff.

CORPORATION OF ST. MARY AND ST. NICOLAS.

Southern Division.

	School	a.	b.
	Lancing (1848)	a. 7,050	b. 275
	Hurstpierpoint (1851)	a. 5,847	b. 149
	Bloxham (1860)	a. 3,050	b. 143
	Ardingly (1858)	a. 11,374	b. 290
G.	St. Michael's, Bognor (1844)	a. 2,594	b. 149

Midland Division.

	School	a.	b.
	Denstone (1873)	a. 6,247	b. 320
	Ellesmere (1879)	a. 3,400	b. 215
	Worksop (1895)	a. 3,550	b. 380
G.	Abbot's Bromley (1874)	a. 4,830	b. 310 boarders.
G.	Llanfairfechan	a. 2,602	b. 121

Western Division.

	King's College, Taunton (1897 re-opened)	a. —	b. 189
G.	*Heatherton Park*	a. —	b. 78
G.	*St. Clare's, Polwithen, Penzance* (C. of E. High School, 1889, Woodard from 1928).	a. —	b. 113

Northern Division.

G.	*Queen Margaret's* (1901), *Scarborough*	a. 1,677	b. 143
G.	*Queen Ethelburga's* (1912), *Harrogate*	a. 863	b. 146
G.	*Queen Mary's (Preparatory) Helmsley* (1925)	a. 249	b. 62

(The figures in brackets refer to the date of foundation.) *a.* No. entered since commencement. *b.* No. on books. *G.* indicates a Girls' School: *statistics* are up to *1937* only. How few statesmen have left a legacy to compare with this work of " an inconspicuous and poorly educated curate of ninety years ago."

[14] High Schools at Dulwich, Guildford, Hull, Atherley School (Southampton), Sunderland, Surbiton, Streatham College, York College were in the Company's hands in 1937.

Localized schools. High schools at Durham; Bury St. Edmunds; Newcastle-upon-Tyne; Northampton; St. Aidan's, Stroud Green; Abbey School, Reading; Derby; St. Albans; Gt. Yarmouth; Kensington Park High School (transferred to Mary's College, 1901). *Transferred to Local Education Authority.* Richmond and Wigan High Schools, both in 1905.

[15] pp. 507 ff. of the 1937 edition.

[16] Kirk, *op. cit.*, pp. 128 ff.

[17] See *County Education,* 1861.

[18] Royal Commn. on Secondary Educn., 1895, Vol. V, pp. 503–5.

[19] Schools Inquiry Commn., Vol. VII, pp. 95 ff.

[20] Royal Commn. on Secondary Educn., 1895, Vol. V, p. 505.

[21] pp. 151–6. (See also Schools Inquiry Commission, Vol. IV, pp. 685 ff.)

[22] p. 154.

[23] Schools Inquiry Commission, Vol. IV, pp. 687–90.

[24] *Ibid.*, Vol. V, pp. 685 ff.

[25] Royal Commn. on Secondary Educn., 1895, Vol. VII, p. 26.

[26] *Ibid.*, 27.

[27] *Ibid.*, pp. 67–8, and *ibid.*, Vol. IX, pp. 330 ff.

[28] *Ibid.*, pp. 294 ff.

[29] *Ibid.*, pp. 306 ff.

[30] *Ibid.*, pp. 238 ff.

[31] Schools Inquiry Commission, Vol. VII, p. 75.

[32] Royal Commn. on Secondary Educn., 1895, Vol. VI, p. 92.

[33] Acland and Llewellyn Smith: *Studies in Secondary Education,* p.197.

[34] Schools Inquiry Commn. Vol. XIV, pp. 471 ff.

[35] Royal Commn. on Secondary Educn., Vol. VI, pp. 162 ff.

[36] *Ibid.*, pp. 362–4.

[37] *Ibid.*, p. 164.

[38] See his *Middle Class Education. Scheme of the West of England Examination and Prizes* (1857), and some remarks by the Rev. W. Tuckwell: *Reminiscences of Oxford* (1901), pp. 88–89.

[39] See p. 53 of this essay.

[40] " . . . it is certain that a much better education can now be obtained in a National School for twopence a week than in a middle school for one or two shillings a week ": *Edin. Review,* July, 1861, quoted by J. W.

Adamson—"English Education, 1789–1902," p. 225. See "National Society Middle Class School Committee Report, Class Lists, and Examination Papers for 1871."

[41] 1. Burgh Middle School was a proprietory school under the bishop, the Lord Lieutenant and the two archdeacons, founded in 1863. It had 45 boys, of whom 21 were boarders.

2. Christ Church, Albany Street, was a much inferior school opened in 1853 for the sons of tradesmen, and had 45 day boys.

3. Durham House, Clapham Common, was a superior private venture school that dated back to 1809. Its 70 boys included 40 boarders.

4. An old endowed school, Farnham Grammar School, dating from the seventeenth century, had 62 boys, of whom 14 were boarders. (It now flourishes as a state aided school.)

5. Milton-next-Gravesend, Parish of Holy Trinity, had a middle class commercial school for 70 boys set up in 1865.

6. Kennington, St. John's, Middle Class School, dated from 1868 and provided for its 110 day boys.

7. Lowther Grammar School resembled Farnham: it was a seventeenth century foundation. It had 45 boys (some boarders).

8. New Brompton, Chatham, St. Mark's, was begun in 1864, and had 80 day scholars.

9. Reading, St. Lawrence Middle Class School, of 1870, had 70 boys, of whom ten were boarders.

10. St. Mary's College, Peckham, was started in 1868 and was a self-supporting and "semi-public school" for 200 boys, of whom thirty were boarders.

[42] Spens Report, p. 26. For Lichfield, see above, p. 22; for Chester and Lincoln see table of Training Colleges from 1845 Committee of Council Report, pp. 146, 147.

[43] Schools Inquiry Commission, Vol. IV, pp. 602 ff.

[44] See Acland and Llewellyn Smith: *Studies in Secondary Education,* 1892, p. 193.

[45] Royal Commn. on Secondary Educn., 1895, Vol. IX, pp. 392 ff.

[46] Royal Commn. on Secondary Educn., 1895, Vol. IX, pp. 282 ff.

[47] *Ibid.,* Vol. VII, pp. 154–8.

[48] Schools Inquiry Commission, Vol. IV, pp. 605 ff.

[49] "Report from the Select Committee on Education of the Poorer Classes in England and Wales" (1838), p. 27, has a tribute to Mr. Wigram's very superior infant school in Vere Street.

[50] Cf. the naïve acceptance by the Cross Commission, 2nd Report, 1887, p. xiii, of "Mr. Thomas Smyth, Representative of the Working Classes, Chelsea."

[51] Schools Inquiry Commission, Vol. X, p. 209. It is claimed that the Girls' Public Day Schools Trust took its ideas from this school.

[52] Cross Commission, 2nd Report, 1887, p. 94.

[53] pp. 157 ff.

[54] Committee of Council Report, 1846, p. 370.

[55] *Ibid.,* p. 374.

[56] *Ibid.,* pp. 384–5.

[57] Maltby, *op. cit.,* p. 65. The Committee of Council Report, 1847–8, Vol. II, pp. 33–4, has an account of the Manchester Church Education Society.

[58] Committee of Council Report, 1856–7, p. 270.

[59] See the Committee of Council Report, 1855–6, pp. 34 ff.; Bartley, *op. cit.,* pp. 156–9; Schools Inquiry Commn., Vol. IV, pp. 198 ff.

III. CRITICISM AND SURVEY

[1] This extreme statement of a view quite commonly taken is extracted from Sir Percy Jackson's Foreword to J. Corlett: *A Survey of the Financial Aspects of Elementary Education* (1929). Cf. Professor Claude Jenkins: *Frederick Denison Maurice and the New Reformation*, p. 62.

"But we shall not succeed in understanding the conditions unless attention is resolutely concentrated upon the position as it was rather than upon what it ought to have been judged by anachronistic modern standards. Nor was there any more general agreement as to what was to be taught than as to who were to teach and who were to receive the instruction and to be educated."

[2] The National Society reports stress the volume of church effort, while the inspectors' reports in the Comm. of Council Reports are valuable for individual schools and first-hand " field " information.

[3] See above, note 6, p. 127.

[4] There are exceptions. The theological mind of the Master of Corpus can hardly be seen in the Spens Report!

[5] For the evidence offered by Mr. W. E. Forster himself to the effect that the poor people of this country demanded a religious education, see National Education Union, Verbatim Report, pp. 206, cols. 2 ff., also *ibid.*, pp. 242, cols. 1 ff.

[6] Cf. the vital part that " religion " played in Charles Booth's *Survey of London Life and Labour* (1889–91), with the *New Survey* (1930) by the London School of Economics.

[7] Real teaching on the nature of the church and the sacraments is almost entirely confined to the minority of the poor who go to a church elementary school and the social strata sending their children to public schools. The intermediate secondary school class falls outside these groups.

[8] Cf. F. J. E. Raby in *History*, June 1939, pp. 64–5: " He would perhaps have some sympathy with Professor Powicke, who said recently, ' Only those who accept the dogma of the divinity of Christ as the central fact in a long process of divine revelation can escape bewilderment in the contemplation of the spread of Christianity, which has been so unlike other religions in its claim to penetrate and control the whole of life. The historian who must discard dogmas, betrays his bewilderment at every step. He tends to explain the history of the Church by explaining it away.' "

[9] Report, Vol. I, pp. 295, 297.

[10] Reference to Hansard of March 25th, 1862: " The Revised Code. Distribution of Grants—Motion for Committee " may well cause the impartial reader to ask himself whether the State was as yet fit to be entrusted with much control of popular education.

[11] *Church Education Since 1870*, p. 20.

APPENDIX I

" A DISSECTION of the Queries on the Amount of Religious Education and Instruction circulated by Lord John Russell." 1838. " By a Clergyman of South Wilts."

This pamphlet is a masterpiece almost worthy of Swift, and is mentioned here because it exposes, with incisive and scornful competence, the Government's illogical Classification of schools. This latter underrated the church's position.

The schools were to be classified as

    (1)   National Society Schools.
    (2)   British and Foreign School Society Schools.
    (3)   Other religious denominations.

All schools belonging to the church and not in union with the National Society should be placed in column (3), and be credited to the Nonconformists, a double falsification of the true position.

(See *Reminiscences, chiefly of Oriel College and the Oxford Movement,* 2nd Edn., 1882, p. 6. Here the author, the Rev. Thos. Mozley, says that he wrote the work and Newman regretted he had not received the pamphlet for his *British Critic.)*

APPENDIX II

1. That the children be instructed in the Holy Scripture and in the Liturgy and Catechism of the Established Church.

2. With respect to such instruction, the schools are to be subject to the superintendence of the parochial clergyman.

3. The children are to be regularly assembled for the purpose of attending divine service in the parish church, or other place of worship under the Establishment, unless such reason be assigned for their non-attendance as is satisfactory to the managers of the school.

4. The masters and mistresses are to be members of the Church of England.

5. A report on the state and progress of the schools is to be made, at Christmas in every year, to the Diocesan Board, the District Society or the National Society, and the schools are, with the consent of the managers, to be periodically inspected by persons appointed either by the bishop of the diocese, the National Society, or the Diocesan Board of Education.

   (There is also a provision that disputes between managers and clergy are to be finally decided by the bishop.)

APPENDIX III

EDUCATIONAL IDEALS OF THE NATIONAL SOCIETY

(From the Society's Annual Report, 1847: pp. 2 ff.)

" THE fundamental principle of this Society—a principle which now seems happily to be very generally recognized and approved—has ever been—that all education, deserving the name, must be based upon Religion; and that education, in its full and proper sense, cannot rightly be said to be carried on, where definite religious belief and religious principle do not pervade the whole teaching of a school. Your Committee believe that much fewer persons than formerly are now to be found who would contend that it is not necessary to education that special religious instruction (as it was called) should be given in a school; and who think that the children of persons of all religious tenets may safely be placed in the same school, under the same teacher, and be taught those general truths of religion only on which all their parents are agreed. Against such a notion the National Society has always entered its earnest protest; contending, that to profess to be educating a child, and yet to make nought, or to make light, of definite religious belief and principle, is to engender in youth the most fatal habit of mind and thought, and to sap the foundation of all religion in the breast. The children brought up in such a school would breathe an atmosphere of hesitancy and doubt on almost all matters of Revelation: and the necessary tendency of such a scheme would seem to be, to produce in their young minds a coldness towards religion, if not to stamp them with a positive scepticism.

" Again, others have said that while they agreed with the National Society in rejecting the notion of placing children in a school where the master should so contrive to generalize religion, as to inculcate nothing except what men of all forms and shades of religious opinion might be brought to agree upon, yet that another scheme was feasible, for educating together all children, irrespective of religious tenets; namely, that the schoolmaster should professedly and distinctly impart secular and literary instruction only; and that certain fixed

153

hours should be set apart, at which the ministers of religion might attend, in separate rooms, to teach religious belief and religious principle. To this plan the Society has ever opposed its leading principle—that education is not education, unless religion is, throughout, its pervading essence. For education means much more than instruction. To educate a child the master must do more than impart certain lessons. The master should be more than a clever expert teacher. You want to bring mind in contact with mind, the mature mind of a religious Master in contact with the impressible mind of his Scholar. You want the innermost spirit of the Man to hold converse with the innermost spirit of the Child. You want the heart of the child to catch some of the holy fire of religion which should burn in the breast of the master, and breathe through all his actions. Religion is not only imparted in set lessons, but in the whole course of school discipline, by example, by gesture, by look, by the turn of a phrase, by a kind of mental contagion which may be understood, though it can hardly be described. To use the eloquent words of a living Bishop of our Church, ' Dogmatic theology has been, alas, too often made most secular instruction : ciphering may be made religious.' Do what you will, the child *will* look up to the schoolmaster as his Educator; and the school-master will mainly contribute to form, not only the future mechanic, but the future *man*. And shall the schoolmaster be one who is forbidden to name the name of Christ? Nay, if you would give the child a chance of growing up a religious being, the master must be a person who *is* religious. He must be one whose spirit will prompt and urge him, upon every occasion, to seize the moment when the heart of an erring child is warm and malleable, for impressing it indelibly with some of the touching words, or with the still more touching example, of our Saviour. No one has such opportunities as the schoolmaster for doing this. But if the master is not permitted, nay bound, thus to bring forward the doctrines and precepts of Christianity, and to found all his rules and his discipline upon them—if these things are not interwoven naturally with the daily school routine, but are merely taught in a cold, set, formal way, at stated intervals—then, at the very best, the child insensibly learns to look upon religion as a medicinal drug to be occasionally resorted to, instead of regarding it as the very bread of life. Religion has, indeed, its truths and its mysteries, which should be taught to the child at stated times, and exhibited to him as matters for his docile belief and humble reverence. But it is altogether unsound to make that branch of religion which relates to the working of one's own mind and consciousness, to the regulation of the thoughts and acts, a by-part in a child's education, to teach it as a thing existing by itself, and standing apart from the general interests and concerns of man. In the case of every man who is brought within the knowledge of Christianity, religion is at all times working at his heart, and taking a part in his every act, bringing a savour of life unto life, or of death unto death. The living energy of religion is requisite for all men, but especially for the poor; it alone can enable them to transmute their hard necessities into duties, and be content in the place of happiness to look for blessedness. On these grounds your Committee have the greatest satisfaction in reiterating their firm conviction, that the Society's plan of basing education upon a definite religious ground, and of placing a master in every school who shall be expected to inculcate freely his religious feelings and opinions, in contradistinction to the two plans above referred to, is at length duly appreciated throughout the country.

" There is another principle of the Society in the matter of education, the soundness of which may be said to have become recognized in the important discussions and events of the past year; namely, that while it is the duty of the State to assist religious bodies in providing the machinery of education, yet, that the more immediate and direct education of the people, the training of their hearts and minds, must depend upon the voluntary and benevolent energies of those who are actuated to undertake the task from a sense of religious duty. Indeed, this principle clearly results from the above-mentioned principle, that education must be based upon religion. For if the education of the people depends, as it certainly does, not so much on the bare lessons given and instruction imparted as upon the *idea* under which their education is taken up, and the *spirit* in which it is treated and carried on, then it is evident, that in this country the State, at the present time, is not fully competent to the work. It might instruct, but it could not educate. It might cause the people to acquire much useful information, to become early sensible of the temporal importance of learning their trades, and of being decent and upright members of society, but it could not imbue them betimes with the solemn feeling that they have souls to be saved. This impression can be duly produced in the minds of children only when they feel, with more or less consciousness, that their educators approach them not more with zeal for their temporal than for their eternal interests.

"The two great principles now referred to—first, that it is essential to education that religion pervade the whole teaching of a school; and secondly, that the main direction of education should be left in the hands of those who would be prompted to approach and handle it from a care for the immortal souls of the children—have been practically recognized in the recent very important minutes of Council, bearing date 25th August, and 21st December, 1846."

APPENDIX IV

RECOMMENDATIONS

OF THE

JOINT CONFERENCE OF ANGLICANS AND EVANGELICAL FREE
CHURCHMEN

ON

RELIGIOUS EDUCATION

Held at intervals from 1937 to 1941

EARLY in 1937 an unofficial Conference between certain
Members of the Anglican Church and of the Evangelical Free
Churches was arranged to consider the present position of
Religious Education in England, and to suggest measures for
its fuller recognition and improvement. The Rev. Dr. J.
Scott Lidgett was appointed Chairman, with the Rev. R. E.
Parsons as Hon. Secretary.

In December, 1938, a Report was issued and widely circulated to members of Public Bodies and of Denominations
and others interested. The Conference unanimously and
strongly urged

(1) That, in addition to the practice of corporate worship,
    instruction in the Christian Faith should have its due
    place among the subjects that are recognized by the com-
    munity and by all education authorities as demanding
    reverent and intellectual study in the colleges and schools
    of the country.

(2) That Teachers in all types of schools should be
    adequately equipped to give to Religious instruction this
    place both in the work of the school and in the minds of
    the scholars.

(3) That scholars should be carefully taught in graded
    courses suitably adapted to the different stages of their
    education.

The following recommendations were submitted for the
consideration of all those responsible for National Education
in all its branches.

Recommendations:—

The Universities

(i) That in the judgment of the Conference it is desirable that in all Universities a Degree Course in Divinity should be available and also that Religious Knowledge should be an optional subject in one or more of the Honours Degree Courses, e.g., General Arts, History, English, for the benefit of those preparing for the teaching profession. [As amended, 1941.]

(ii) That in all cases instruction in Religious Knowledge should be provided and a diploma or certificate in the same be made available. [As amended, 1941.]

(iii) Recognizing the great value of the Lambeth Diploma in Theology available to women, the Conference desires that the same advantage should be extended to men.

(iv) That in view of the great importance of provision being made for teachers to carry on their studies in order to equip themselves in knowledge of the Bible as well as in methods of teaching it, it is very desirable that extra-mural lectures should be made available for them by all the Universities and University Colleges of the Country. Such work may well be supplemented by the arrangement of Summer Schools.

(v) That there should be included on the staff of every University Training Department a specialist in biblical knowledge and methods of teaching it.

(vi) That, as in the case of certain Universities at present, the part of the Diploma Examination dealing with the teaching of special subjects should include the teaching of Religious Knowledge as one of the options.

The Training Colleges

(i) Due place should be found on the timetable in order to allow adequate time for the religious instruction of all students who desire to take advantage of the courses provided.

(ii) That for such teaching adequate arrangements should be made.

(iii) That practical help should be given to students concerning the methods of giving religious instruction.

(iv) That there should be more general provision for teachers to continue their biblical and other religious studies after they have left college. Also that suitable libraries should be provided and kept up to date by all Local Authorities for the use of teachers.

SECONDARY SCHOOLS

(i) That the attention of the responsible bodies be called to the conditions of religious teaching in Preparatory, Public and Secondary Schools, and that they be urged to use every possible means of encouraging Headmasters and Headmistresses to promote the teaching of religious subjects in their schools.

(ii) That while fully aware of the enormous and steadily increasing pressure of examination subjects the Conference is convinced that the true welfare of boys and girls cannot be secured without continuity of religious education to the close of their school life.

(iii) That with this object it is desirable that an ordered scheme of instruction should be available for guidance in co-ordinating the teaching given in Preparatory, Public and Secondary Schools in order to secure a steady development in the knowledge of Scripture throughout the school life.

(iv) That in order to bring the subject up to the level of the other subjects, and not as a substitute for religious exercises, it is important that in all schools there should be teachers willing and equipped to give religious instruction.

ELEMENTARY SCHOOLS

(i) The Conference emphasizes the importance of the use in all provided schools and for general religious instruction in non-provided schools, of Agreed Syllabuses—agreed in the sense that the bodies concerned with the preparation and selection of them should include representatives of teachers as well as of the Churches.

(ii) The Conference trusts that those Local Education Authorities that have not yet introduced Agreed Syllabuses, will, without further delay, adopt those of approved educational excellence.

(iii) That in order to secure continuity of distinctive religious instruction for children of parents who desire it, suitable arrangements may be made where practicable under the provision of Section 13 of the Education Act, 1936, and the Anson Bye-law.

(iv) The value of securing a greater elasticity of the time-table for giving of religious instruction is urged.

(v) The Conference is impressed with the desirability of the avoidance of any kind of pressure upon the teacher to give religious instruction if he has any hesitation in his own mind about it. (This to be without prejudice to the teacher concerned.)

(vi) It is desirable that all teachers who give religious instruction should be qualified by attendance at such courses as have been outlined above.

The Report and Recommendations gained wide and favourable publicity and received consideration by many of the Bodies chiefly concerned.

The Unofficial Conference has become recognized by the National Society (Central Council of the Church for Religious Education) and by the Free Church Federal Council, the present membership being stated below.

Resulting from many further consultations these supplementary recommendations have been adopted:—

The Training Colleges.

(v) That Religious Knowledge be included among the optional subjects which count for the Joint Board Teachers' Certificate.

Secondary Schools.

That in order to establish the principle that Divinity should be taught in the Secondary Schools of the Country and made continuous throughout the pupil's school life, the Board of Education be asked to use its influence with Local Education Authorities in regard to the following points:—

(v) That the practice whereby Divinity takes its place with the other subjects and activities of the curriculum as a subject of inspection in Secondary Schools should be extended as widely as possible.

(vi) That as far as possible there should be Divinity Specialists on the staffs of Secondary Schools, as generally indicated in the Spens Report on Secondary Education.

(vii) That encouragement should be given to teachers in Secondary Schools to qualify for the post of Divinity Specialist, by giving them leave of absence for the purpose of attending courses, by grants towards the cost of fees for such courses and towards travelling expenses.

Elementary Schools.

(vii) In order that the efficiency of religious instruction should be equal to that of any other subject, supervision over the curriculum and teaching should be exercised, whether through H.M. Inspector or L.E.A. Inspectors.

(viii) That Local Education Authorities be urged to ensure that in all schools there are sufficient teachers willing and qualified to give religious instruction in accordance with the syllabus in use under the Authorities concerned and, in order to maintain a supply of such teachers, Local Education Authorities be urged to increase the number of their courses in this subject and to facilitate and encourage attendance by their staffs at these or similar courses.

(ix) That Section 10 of the Code of Regulations for Public Elementary Schools be amended so as to permit amongst the items enumerated upon the timetable a short period for an opening service, and that H.M. Inspectors should be instructed accordingly.

In view of the widespread public interest in the question the members of the Conference have set forth in this document their Recommendations of three years ago, together with those since adopted, and an indication of action taken and encouraging progress made. They earnestly call for the united activities of the Christian forces of the nation towards securing a more efficient Christian training for character and citizenship in schools and colleges so far as post-war legislation can help to provide it.

Correspondence in connexion with these Recommendations should be addressed to the Hon. Secretary of the Joint

Conference, Canon A. L. Woodard, The Manor, Swaffham Prior, Cambridge.

COPIES MAY BE OBTAINED (1/1 per dozen, post free) FROM THE FOLLOWING SOCIETIES :—

Church of England.

The National Society (Central Council of the Church for Religious Education),
    69, Great Peter Street,
        Westminster, S.W. 1.
Church Tutorial Classes Association,
    69, Great Peter Street,
        Westminster, S.W. 1.

Free Church Federal Council,
    27, Tavistock Square, London, W.C. 1.
Methodist Education Department,
    Westminster Training College,
        Southfield House,
            Westbury-on-Trym, Bristol.

Interdenominational.

The Institute of Christian Education,
    Badsey, Evesham, Worcs.
The Student Christian Movement,
    " Annandale," North End Road,
        Golders Green, N.W. 11.
The Christian Education Movement,
    (Secretary, Canon F. A. Cockin),
        1, Amen Court, London, E.C. 4.

MEMBERS OF JOINT CONFERENCE :—

Church of England :—

The Bishop of Grimsby ; Canon G. D. Barker ; Mr. E. R. J. Hussey ; Sir Robert E. Martin ; Sir Walter Moberly ; Canon Tissington Tatlow ; Canon A. L. Woodard (Hon. Secretary).

Free Churches :—

Rev. Dr. J. Scott Lidgett (Chairman) ; Mr. Arthur Black ; Rev. W. T. Elmslie ; Rev. Dr. A. E. Garvie ; Rev. Dr. A. W. Harrison ; Rev. Dr. W. T. Whitley ; Rev. Dr. H. B. Workman ; Rev. Dr. B. A. Yeaxlee.

STATISTICAL APPENDIX

(a) STATISTICS FROM THE NATIONAL SOCIETY'S SURVEY OF 1846–7

SCHOOLS*: 20,350 *(Free Schools:* 6,659. *Pay Schools:* 13,691).

Sunday and Week-day	10,788
Week-day only	5,410
Sunday only	3,641
Sunday and Week-day evening	330
Week-day evening	181

SCHOLARS: 1,301,863 (net figure after deducting duplicate entries).

Sunday and Week-day	*Boys*	336,459	
	Girls	308,806	645,265
Week-day only	*Boys*	122,506	
	Girls	107,211	229,717
Sunday only	*Boys*	189,177	
	Girls	215,382	404,559
Sunday and Week-day evening	*Boys*	6,502	
	Girls	5,886	12,388
Week-day evening	*Boys*	7,147	
	Girls	2,787	9,934

Grand Totals: 661,791 Boys: 640,072 Girls.

SCHOOLROOMS: 20,062.

Legally secured	6,110
Virtually secured	4,467
Not secured rooms in dames' cottages	3,222
Portions of church, incl. vestry	1,602

TEACHERS' RESIDENCES: 8,446.

TEACHERS:

Paid Masters and Mistresses	21,560
Monitors	4,051
Gratuitous Masters and Mistresses in Sunday Schools	49,635

* For purposes of comparison with later figures, e.g. those of 1861 (pp. 165 ff. below), this should read as "schoolrooms," but it is a figure of no real significance.

CASH EXPENDITURE.

Grants made by the National Society for
    Building Schools in the years 1811–47   £278,691
Cost of yearly Salaries to Teachers, but
    excluding monitors   £568,448
Expense of School Maintenance   £802,460 p.a.

The National Society's grants represent only a small fraction of the total cost of building parish schools.

(b) STATISTICS OF THE NATIONAL SOCIETY'S SURVEY OF
1856–7

SCHOOLS : (p. ii. " it has been found impossible to ascertain correctly the number of distinct schools from which returns have been returned ").

SCHOLARS : 1,599,121.

Sunday and Week-day	Boys	326,160	
	Girls	312,360	638,520
Week-day only	Boys	174,350	
	Girls	140,680	
	Infants	181,311	496,341
Sunday only	Boys	191,799	
	Girls	219,887	411,934
Week-day evening	Boys	38,761	
	Girls	13,565	52,326

TEACHERS :

Masters	7,247
Assistant Masters	595
Mistresses	12,138
Assistant Mistresses	1,243
Male pupil teachers and paid monitors	4,233
Female ,, ,, ,, ,, ,,	4,841

CASH EXPENDITURE :

Endowment	£107,425
School Pence	£217,052
Subscriptions and other sources	£332,439
	£656,916

This compares with a Government grant of £629,056 for the country's elementary education.

The following figures supplied as representative of the composition of school management committees may be cited :

43% by clergy and committee
37% „   „   alone
 9% „   „   and chief landowner
 5% „   chief landowner and family
 3% „   lay committee
 3% „   proprietor of neighbouring works.

Her Majesty's Inspector says that a great advantage of the voluntary system is that the schools are placed in the hands of those who take the truest interest in it. " No state system could secure this " (Comm. of Council Report, 1858–9, p. 99). This survey does *not* include Nonconformist Schools, Church Boarding Schools, Preparatory Schools, Workhouse Schools, Orphan Asylums or Grammar Schools as such, but it *does* include *Church* Dames' Schools. (N.B. pp. ii–iii for marked diminution in dames' schools due to improved parochial schools.) ". . . in 1839, the Dean and Chapter of Canterbury contributed to the support of a dame school which the Vicar of Herne Hill had established at his own expense at Dunkirk in Kent." (Board of Education Consultative Committee Report on Infant and Nursery Schools, p. 4.)

The following comparison is made on page iii—" In 1847 the estimated population of England and Wales, the Isle of Man and the Channel Islands was 17,224,148 ; and the total number of children under instruction in Church schools, including week-day, Sunday and evening schools was returned as 1,422,569 or about 8·259% of the entire population. In 1857 the estimated population was 19,422,495 and the total number of children under instruction in Church schools has been reported to be 1,672,445 or about 8·611% of the whole population." The apparent discrepancy between this figure of 1,672,445 and that of the Newcastle Commission quoted in the next section, 1,187,086, is explained by the former's inclusion of Sunday and Evening Scholars, who could not, of course, be regarded as receiving a satisfactory education.

(c) National Society's Jubilee Figures
" The Work of the National Society during half a century "
CASH EXPENDITURE.

   Grants made to Schools and for Teachers'
     Residences   £367,831

	Brought forward	£367,831
Expenses attendant on Raising and Disbursing Funds and diffusing general information		81,000
Grants towards cost of erecting Training Institutions		55,549
Cost of maintaining the National Society's Training Establishments		219,470
Cost of Organizing Masters		9,000
Cost of Establishing and Maintaining Metropolitan and Provincial Depositories	nearly	10,000
Cost of Conducting Inquiries as to the State of Church Schools		3,000
		£745,850

SCHOOLS, SCHOLARS AND TEACHERS.

Number of Schools in Union	nearly	12,000
Number of Elementary Schoolrooms in connexion with the Church	nearly	19,000
Number of Teachers supplied		8,500
Number of Scholars in Schools in Union		1,100,000

The Newcastle Commissioners (1861) reported (Vol. I, p. 55) as follows :

Description of School.	*Centesimal proportion of the Scholars educated by the respective Denominations.*	
	Week-day Schools	*Sunday Schools*
Church of England	76·2	45·8
British	9·7	–
Roman Catholic	5·52	1·5
Wesleyan (Original Connexion)	3·91	19·0
Baptist	·7	6·7
Unitarian	·3	·6
Jewish	·2	–
Calvinistic Methodists	·2	4·7
Society of Friends	·2	–
Presbyterians in England	·2	–
Primitive Methodists	·09	5·7
Methodist New Connexion	·1	2·2
United Methodist Free Churches	·08	2·6
Undefined Presbyterians	·2	–
Other	·3	–
Totals in reckoning	1,553,212	2,388,397

Newcastle Commission, Vol. I, p. 592 has a useful comparative table of

Numbers of Week-day Schools and Scholars

School.	Week-day Schools, i.e. Departments.	Scholars. Male.	Female.	Total.	Av. No. of Scholars in School.
Ch. of England	19,549	624,104	562,982	1,187,086	60·7
British	1,131	89,843	61,162	151,005	113·5
Roman Catholic	743	41,678	44,188	85,866	115·5
Wesleyan Old Connexion	445	35,887	23,986	59,873	134·5
Congregational	388	18,143	15,020	33,163	85·4
Baptist	144	5,102	4,286	9,388	65·2

No other denomination had above 54 schoolrooms. The number of church schoolrooms and scholars, it may be noted, is in excess of that claimed by the National Society.

(d) STATISTICS OF NATIONAL SOCIETY'S SURVEY OF 1866–7

Part I has reference to parishes which have *not* separate church parochial or National schools. Some of these have church cottage or dames' schools, while others look to adjoining parishes. The deciding factor as to whether a school is needed or not is obviously that of population or the maximum distance the children may have to walk to school.

Part II gives a census of Church of England schools— week-day, Sunday, evening—and details of such matters as the number of teachers and their qualifications in the way of training, the income of the school, etc. (p. 4). " As the proportion of Church week-day and night schools annually aided out of the Parliamentary grant for education is a most important element in ascertaining the extent to which annual State aid has, or has not, covered the country at large, we have stated it, and supplied other information bearing upon the subject." The Committee of Council can only publish details of schools that they actually assist, and cannot possibly know how many other schools exist. This information compiled by the National Society has been moved for as a Parliamentary Paper by the Duke of Marlborough in the Lords " (see Hansard, March 8th, 1869, (Third series, Vol. CXCIV, page 815, cols. 1 & 2) where His Grace quotes from the survey).

M

Part III is a comparison between this and previous surveys.

Table I

Parishes without schools, but supplied with education in adjoining parishes, in England and Wales   1,355

Of these, 508 parishes have fewer than 100 people, but 10 parishes have between 3,500 and 5,000 souls.

In large towns (e.g. Exeter, York, Norwich) there are "central" and in London "ward" schools set up for serving several adjoining parishes.

Table III

This gives details of the maximum distances children must walk to reach their schools in adjoining parishes.

The children in 383 parishes have to walk less than 1 mile.

,,	,,	,,	9	,,	,,	,,	,, between $2\frac{1}{2}$ and 3 miles.
,,	,,	,,	16	,,	,,	,,	,, 3 ,, $3\frac{1}{2}$,,
,,	,,	,,	1 parish	,,	,,	,,	,, $3\frac{1}{2}$,, 4 ,,
,,	,,	,,	0 parishes	,,	,,	,,	4 miles.

But these measurements are from parish boundary to the adjoining parish school, and a walk of some distance must have been often entailed before the children reached their parish boundary. This rural problem still persists.

The National Society claims that "educational destitution" is only occasionally found, and where this is so it is due to the fact that the chief landowner will not act, or the parson has only a "limited income," or there is no extraneous aid. But this explanation did not help the children!

In 338 parishes there is neither a separate church school nor convenient adjoining schools, although there might be other voluntary schools adequately filling the need.

In 25 parishes there were under 100 souls.

,,	52	,,	,,	,,	between	1,000 and 2,000 souls.
,,	21	,,	,,	,,	,,	3,000 ,, 5,000 ,,
,,	19	,,	,,	,,	above	5,000 souls.

(p. 11) Dames' schools were largely supported by the clergy and the children's pence. Their connexion with the clergy was frequently close. The church catechism was taught in many such schools, the clergy often provided books, and the children were taken to church. The aim of these schools was often to serve as purely infant schools and not to make a profit.

In 662 parishes there are only Dames' Schools, and of these,
,, 106   ,,   ,,   were under 100 souls
,, 351   ,,   ,,   ,,   between 100 and 300 souls.
(p. 14)   The following statistics are from *Part II*.
Week-day Schools (England only).

Schools	11,261
Scholars	1,433,239
Scholars in average daily attendance	1,029,376

The Registrar General's estimate of population in 1866
was 20,367,608.
% of est. population on registers was 7 (1 in 14·1)
% of est. population in av. daily attendance was 5 (1 in 19·7)
   These figures only include specifically church schools or
dames' schools controlled by clergymen, as in 1858.   (p. 15)
Av. daily attendance in England and Wales was 71·8% of
number on registers.

Night Schools (p. 17) (England only).

Schools	4,128
Night Scholars on register	144,470
in av. attendance	96,165
% of est. popn. on registers	·7
% of est. popn. in av. attendance	·5

On p. 19 we have some vital figures that we may read to-day
as statistics of achievement in the night schools in the sense
the National Society intended : people were now being
educated at night who had not previously been educated in
the day schools.   (The Manchester Education Aid Society
initiated the work of a " school attendance officer " by seeking
out children not attending school.   (Committee of Council
Report, 1866–7, pp. 40–1.)   This body was interdenominational : for its history see Maltby : *Manchester and the
Movement for National Elementary Education,* Chapter VIII,
pp. 95 ff.)   It is probably fairer to attribute this state of things
not to defects in the voluntary system, but to economic causes
for parents could not afford to keep their children at the day
schools in the " Hungry Forties."   The following figures are
interesting.

Number of Night Schools making returns	1,051
,, ,, Scholars on their registers	41,252
,, ,, foregoing who have never been at Week-day Schools	3,082
	(7·4%)

" It should be borne in mind, however, that night schools are attended in general, not by children, but by young persons, and sometimes even by men and women, in whose early days week-day schools were less common than they are at the present moment." It is important to note (p. 20) that attendance was expected on each of the three (sometimes five) nights on which the school was generally open. The average fee in rural districts was threepence per week : in urban districts, generally sixpence, but in some instances it rose to one shilling. The staff was mainly voluntary, or had only one paid teacher.

Sunday Schools (p. 21) (England only).

| Schools | 11,078 |
| Scholars | 1,209,413 |

in average attendance 896,084 (74%).

Training of Teachers (p. 24).

Masters and Mistresses	18,751	
Number of above trained	6,520	(34·7%)
,, ,, ,, *certificated*	7,917	(42·2%)

In the case of 168 schools selected for examination there was a total income of £4,518 from the contributions of the following :

169 clergymen	gave £1,782	or £10/10/0 per head.
399 landowners	,, £2,127	,, £5/6/0 ,, ,,
217 occupiers of land	,, £200	,, £0/18/6 ,, ,,
102 householders	,, £181	,, £1/15/6 ,, ,,
141 other persons	,, £228	,, £1/12/4 ,, ,,

" The rental of the 399 landowners mentioned in the above table is £650,000 per annum." The impression given here is further borne out : " A table, prepared from the Returns made to the National Society (see Appendix IV, p. 50) shows that in regard to 2,939 schools the deficit in income supplied by the treasurers of these schools, after all receipts, amounted to no less than £52,777, or an average for each treasurer of £18. The treasurers in the majority of cases are clergymen."

(e) I. Statistics after 1870

Numbers of Elementary Schools in 1874 and 1875

1.	*Church Schools*	8,799	9,449	(+650) + 7·4%
2.	*Nonconformist Schools*	2,042	2,034	(— 8) ·
3.	*Roman Catholic Schools*	567	598	(+ 31) ·
4.	*Board Schools*	838	1,136	(+298) +35·5%

Numbers of Elementary Scholars in 1874 and 1875

1. *Church Schools*   1,117,461   1,175,289   57,828 + 5·1%
2. *Nonconformist*
   Schools   322,633   328,180   5,547
3. *Roman Catholic*
   Schools   100,372   106,426   6,054
4. *Board Schools*   138,298   227,285   88,992 +64·4%

Tests made by H.M. Inspectors give the following average annual grant per head in the schools listed above (1) 12/8½, (2) 13/0¼, (3) 12/0¾, (4) 11/0½, but few would be found to-day who would claim these figures as evidence of the superiority of the voluntary system, however sublime a faith in the powers of examiners they may show.

II.   *Year ended 31st Aug.*

Schools	Accommodation.	Av. Attendance.
	1878	
Church	2,252,794	1,368,029
British, etc.	381,993	234,319
Wesleyan	190,889	117,466
Roman Cath.	226,497	126,305
Board	890,164	559,078
Totals	3,942,337	2,405,197

Schools	Accommodation.	Av. Attendance.
	1879	
Church	2,301,073	1,426,595
British, etc.	385,463	240,920
Wesleyan	196,821	121,049
Roman Cath.	242,403	136,690
Board	1,016,464	669,741
Totals	4,142,224	2,594,995

Schools	Accommodation.	Av. Attendance.
	1880	
Church	2,327,379	1,471,615
British, etc.	386,034	243,012
Wesleyan	196,566	121,408
Roman Cath.	248,140	145,629
Board	1,082,634	769,252
Totals	4,240,753	2,750,916

" In conclusion, I would renew my protest against too decided
an inference from actual statistics as to the progress of
elementary education. As a test of this, the average attendance is a far more reliable guide than the average of passes."
H.M. Inspector's Report in Report of Committee of Council,
1876–7, p. 397.

III. Figures marked * are exclusive of sites costing at least a
million pounds.

VOLUNTARY EXPENDITURE ON CHURCH SCHOOLS AND TRAINING COLLEGES.

Schools	From 1811–70	Since 1870	Total
Buildings	*£6,270,577	*£5,333,595	*£11,604,172
Maintenance	£8,500,000	£6,642,866	£15,142,866
Training Colleges			
Buildings	£194,085	£77,100	£271,185
Maintenance	£185,276	£176,631	£361,907
	£15,149,938	£12,230,192	£27,380,130

IV. We may neglect statistics for accommodation and number
on the registers.

Average Attendance in Day Schools. *Year ended 31st. Aug.*

	1888	1889	1890
Church	1,664,076	1,678,068	1,680,596
British	253,982	256,525	254,873
Wesleyan	130,817	132,873	131,805
Roman Catholic	188,086	190,324	193,285
Board	1,378,006	424,835	457,358
Totals	3,614,967	2,682,625	2,717,917

The following comparative table of voluntary contributions
may be given :

Day Schools. *Voluntary Contributions.* *Year Ended 31st. Aug.*

	1888	1889	1890
Church	£582,081	£582,018	£589,640
British	81,672	83,130	79,723
Wesleyan	15,682	17,191	17,253
Roman Catholic	65,903	67,480	70,911
Totals	£745,338	£749,819	£757,527

(Odd shillings and pence are nowhere quoted.)

Expenditure on Church Schools and Training Colleges

Schools	1811–70	Since 1870	Total
Buildings	£6,270,577	£6,845,512	£13,116,089
Maintenance	8,500,000	12,180,493	20,680,493
Training Colleges			
Buildings	194,085	83,310	277,395
Maintenance	185,276	284,454	469,730
Totals	£15,149,938	£19,393,769	£34,543,707

In church schools in the period 31/8/1870 to 31/8/1890 the following increases are to be noted.

Accommodation in Church Schools—1,285,998
Average attendance   — 836,262

These are, to say the very least, remarkable statistics.

V.   AVERAGE ATTENDANCE IN DAY SCHOOLS
                Year ended 31st Aug.

	1898	1899	1900
Church	1,883,263	1,893,824	1,885,802
British, etc.	230,355	228,142	220,032
Wesleyan	124,971	126,361	125,727
Roman Catholic	246,128	251,768	255,036
Board	2,087,519	2,144,118	2,201,049
Total	4,572,236	4,644,213	4,687,646

VI. *Board of Education Total for the Year of Church Expenditure on Schools, etc.* £624,156. (p. 28 Nat. Soc. Annual Report 1901) *National Society's Statistics of Voluntary Contributions for the Maintenance of Schools and Colleges.*

Income from " other sources for Church Schools, NOT including pence or other public moneys "	£45,197
Maintenance, etc. of Church Training Colleges	14,000
Enlargement and improvement of above	20,000
Cost of Diocesan Inspection of Schools	15,000
,, ,, Examination and Inspection of Church Training Colleges (Religious Knowledge)	1,080
,, ,, Additional Accommodation for at least 12,000 children at £8 per child	96,000
Endowments	122,940
Education Acts	2,500
	£940,873

" No account is taken in the foregoing statement of the cost of maintaining the various central and local organizations for the support and improvement of Church Schools and colleges." It is claimed (p. 29) that since 1811 Churchmen have spent more than £43,000,000, exclusive of site values and privately built schools. On the following page we have a short table :

Church Schools

	Year ending 31.8.1870	Year ending 31.8.1900	Increase.
Accommodation	1,365,080	2,802,525	1,437,445
Average Attendance	844,334	1,885,802	1,041,468

VII.

Grants to Schools for	Buildings	Repairs	Total
1903	£3,361	£ 954	£ 4,415
1904	1,990	3,101	5,091
1905	2,940	4,156	7,096
1906	1,006	2,258	3,534
1907	2,881	13,268	16,159
1908	3,003	6,871	9,874
1909	4,945	4,857	9,702
1910	6,770	3,913	10,683
1911	7,607	4,289	11,896
1912	7,438	4,366	11,804
1913	7,557	3,507	11,064

VIII. The following table of Subscriptions, Donations and Church Collections is of sums additional to those voted by the National Assembly, derived from the voluntary " quotas " of parish and diocese.

1920	£17,000	1934	£18,000
1930	£22,000	1936	£22,000
1932	£18,000	1938	£18,000

(Sums are given to the nearest 000; in 1927 the figure was £23,000)

SELECT BIBLIOGRAPHY OF THE HISTORICAL INTRODUCTION AND OTHER GENERAL BOOKS

1. A. F. Leach : *Educational Charters and Documents, 598–1909. 1911.*
2. do. : *Schools of Medieval England. 1915.*
3. do. : *History of Winchester College. 1899.*
4. do. : *English Schools at the Reformation. 1896.*
5. A. W. Parry : *Education in England in the Middle Ages. 1920.*
6. H. B. Hepple : *Medieval Education in England. 1932.*
7. Foster Watson : *English Grammar Schools to 1660. 1908.*
8. H. Rashdall : (Ed. Powicke and Emden)—*Universities of Europe in the Middle Ages.* 3 Vols. 1936.
9. C. E. Mallett : *History of the University of Oxford.* 3 Vols. 1924–7.
10. *Legacy of the Middle Ages:* article on " Education " by J. W. Adamson. 1926.
11. H. Craik : *State in Relation to Education. 1884.*
12. J. E. G. de Montmorency : *State Intervention in English Education. 1902.*
13. F. Birchenough : *History of Elementary Education.* 1st Edn., 1914; 3rd Edn., 1938.
14. H. McLachlan : *English Education under the Test Acts. 1931.*
15. I. Parker : *Dissenting Academies in England. 1914.*
16. M. G. Jones : *Charity School Movement. 1938.*
17. T. Raymont : *History of the Education of Young Children. 1937.*
18. J. W. Adamson : *An Outline of English Education, 1760–1902.* 1925.
19. do. : *English Education, 1789–1902. 1930.*
20. Frank Smith : *History of English Elementary Education, 1760–1902.* 1931.
21. do. : *Life and Work of Sir James Kay-Shuttleworth. 1923.*
22. H. B. Binns : *A Century of Education, 1808–1908. 1908.*
23. F. Adams : *History of the Elementary School Contest. 1882.*
24. G. C. T. Bartley : *The Schools for the People. 1871.*
25. David Mathew : *Catholicism in England, 1535–1935. 1936.*
26. W. O. B. Allen and Edward McClure : *Two Hundred Years—the History of the S.P.C.K. 1898.*
27. J. L. and B. Hammond : *Town Labourer.* (Many Edns.)
28. do. : *Village Labourer.* (Many Edns.)
29. (Ed.) G. M. Young : *Early Victorian England. 1934.* Vol. I.
    Chapter I by J. H. Clapham : " Works and Wages."
    „ III by R. H. Mottram : " Town Life in London."
    „ IV by J. H. & M. H. Clapham : " Life in the New Towns."
    And in Vol. II, Ch. XV by E. C. P. Lascelles : " Charity."
30. Basil A. Yeaxlee : *Spiritual Values in Adult Education.* 2 Vols. 1925.
31. S. C. Carpenter : *Church and People—1789–1889. 1933.*
32. Bishop Hensley Henson : *The Church of England. 1939.*
33. S. L. Ollard & F. L. Cross : *The Anglo-Catholic Revival in Outline.* 1933. Has valuable bibliographies.
34. Fredk. Maurice : *Life of Frederick Denison Maurice. 1884.*
35. J. H. Overton & F. Relton : *A History of the English Church. From the Accession of George I to the end of the XVIIIth Century. 1714–1800. 1906.*
36. F. Warre Cornish : *The English Church in the Nineteenth Century.* 2 Vols. 1910.

37. G. C. Binyon: *History of the Christian Socialist Movement in England.* 1931.
38. Matthew Arnold: *Culture and Anarchy.* 1869.
39. Dorothy Gardiner: *English Girlhood at School.* 1929.

For Elementary Education Generally

1. *Report of the Select Committee on the State of Education.* 1834.
2. *Report of the Select Committee in England and Wales.* 1835.
3. "Return, showing by Counties, for each Public Elementary School in England and Wales, the average number of scholars in attendance, amount of Government grant for annual maintenance, the the number of children for whom accommodation was provided and the statements of income and expenditure. For the year ending 31st August, 1876." 1877.
4. *Report from the Select Committee on Education of the Poorer Classes in England and Wales.* 1838.
5. *The Annual Report of the Committee of Council upon Education, 1839 to 1898–9* and continued by
6. *The Annual Reports of the Board of Education.*
7. Horace Mann: *Report on Census of 1851.* 1854.
8. Ed. by Alfred Hill: *Essays on Educational Subjects read at the Educational Conference of 1857.* 1857.
9. *Education Commission. Report of the Commissioners appointed to inquire into the State of Popular Education in England.* 1861. (Newcastle Commn.)
10. *Report of the Commissioners appointed to inquire into the Elementary Education Acts. England and Wales. 1866–68.* (Cross Commission.)
11. Sampson Low, Jun. *The Charities of London.* New Edn. Corrected to 1867. 1867.
12. *National Education Union.* A verbatim report, with indices, of the Debate in Parliament during the progress of the Elementary Education Bill, 1870, together with a reprint of the Act. (No date.)
13. *Convocation of the Province of Canterbury*—Lower House: Committee on Primary National Education, Feb. 11th, 1870.
14. Thomas Moore: *Educational Brief on behalf of the Voluntary Schools.* 1890.
15. Church Assembly. *Report of the Commission on Religious Education.* 1929.
16. G. A. N. Lowndes: *Silent Social Revolution.* 1937.
17. S. E. Maltby: *Manchester and the Movement for National Elementary Education, 1800–70.* 1918.
18. Rev. C. Richson: *A Sketch of the Causes, which, in Manchester, induced the abandonment of the Voluntary System in the Support of Schools and the Introduction of the Manchester and Salford Education Bill.* 1851. p. 113.
19. Anon.: *On Self-Supporting Schools of Industry or Mental Discipline.* 1844. p. 36.
20. Anon.: *Poor Rates Reduced by Self-Supporting Reading, Writing, and Agricultural Schools.* Dedicated to Bp. Gilbert of Winchester. 1844. p. 12.
21. F. D. Maurice: *Has the Church or the State the power to Educate the Nation?* 1839.
22.   do.   : *The Educational Question of 1847.*
23.   do.   : (Ed.) *The Educational Magazine.* 1839.
24. Anon. (i.e. Rev. Wm. Rogers): *A Short Account of the St. Thomas', Charterhouse, Schools.* Also Reports of 1851, 1854, 1856, 1857.

25. Rev. H. W. Bellairs: "Work—the Law of God and lot of Man." Sermon. 1852.

26. G. A. Denison: *The Church of England and the Committee of Council on Education.* 1849.

27.   do.   : *The Catechism of the Church of England the Basis of all Teaching in Parish Schools.* 1853.

28.   do.   : *A Brief Account of the National Society.* 1854.

29.   do.   : *Position and Prospects of the National Society.* 1853.

30.   do.   : *Church Schools and State Interference.* 1847

31. Anon.: "Some remarks on a letter addressed by the Rev. Dr. Hook. . . . By one of the Clergy of the Manufacturing District and Parish of Manchester. 1846.

32. J. M. Wilson: *Voluntary Schools and State Education.* 1894.

33. Richd. Burgess: *Educational Statistics, etc.* 1838.

34. W. F. Hook: *On Institutions for Adult Education.* 1852.

35.   do.   : *On Rendering More Efficient the Education of the People.* 1846. (10 Editions.)

36. J. C. Cox: *Plea for Parochial Boarding Schools.* 1850.

37. Henry Moseley: "An Account of the King's Somborne School. Questions answered by Mr. Dicker, now acting as the Ambulatory Schoolmaster, to a Group of Schools in South Devonshire, where the measure proposed by Miss Burdett-Coutts is under trial." May, 1865. (Br. Mus. 8,304,632 (6).)

38. A Clergyman of South Wilts (i.e. Rev. Thos. Mozley): "A Dissection of the Queries on the Amount of Religious Education and Instruction circulated by Lord John Russell." 1838.

39. Richd. Dawes: "Suggestive Hints towards improved Secular Instruction."

40.   do.   : "Hints on an Improved and Self-Paying System of National Education, suggested by the working of the Village School of King's Somborne in Hampshire. (4th Edn., no date.)

41.   do.   : "Remarks occasioned by the Present Crusade against the Educational Plans of the Committee of Council on Education." 1850.

42.   do.   : "An account of the King's Somborne School." (No date.)

43.   do.   : "Schools and other similar Institutions for the Industrial Classes." 1853.

44.   do.   : "Mechanics' Institutes and Popular Education." 1856.

45.   do.   : "Effective Primary Instruction the only sure road to success in the Reading Room, Library and Institutes for Secondary Instruction." 1857.

46. Archdeacon Sinclair: "Charge to the Clergy of Middlesex," 1845. (1st Edn. as a letter to Earl Granville, President of the Committee of Council; 2nd and 3rd Edns. as the Charge; 4th Edn. in 1867—"Remarks on School Rates in England and America.")

47. Horace Mann: "Report of Educational Tour in 1844." 1846.

48. Eden, Hon. & Rev. R. J. (3rd Baron Auckland, Bp. of Bath & Wells): Episcopal "Charges" of 1855, 1858, 1861.

49. Bishop Hinds: "A Letter to Mr. Senior on Supplemental Evening Schools." 1839.

50. Rev. Wm. Gover: "Day School Education in the Borough of Birmingham: our progress, position and needs." 1867.

51. Rev. Wm. Rogers: *Reminiscences.* 1888.

For the National Society

1. Ed. Churton: *Memoir of Joshua Watson.* 2nd Edn., 1863.
2. Dean Robert Gregory: *Elementary Education.* 1895.
3.   do.   : "A Letter to His Grace the Archbishop of Canterbury headed 'Do our National Schools provide Education for all whom they ought to train?'" 1865.
4. *The Annual Reports of the National Society,* 1811 to date. (The Reports of the local associations can in many instances be seen in the National Society library.)
5. *The Monthly Paper,* Jan., 1847—Dec., 1875.
6. *The School Guardian,* Jan., 1876—Oct., 1937.
7. "Results of the Returns to the General Enquiry made by the National Society into the State and Progress of Schools for the Education of the Poor in the Principles of the Established Church during the Years 1846–7 throughout England and Wales." 1849.
8. "Summaries of the Returns to the General Inquiry made by the National Society into the State and Progress of Schools for the Education of the Poor in the Principles of the Established Church during the years 1856–7 throughout England and Wales." 1858.
9. "Statistics of Church of England Schools for the Poor in England and Wales for the years 1866–7." 2nd Edn.
10. "Summary of Replies to the National Society Inquiry as to the Condition and Prospects of Church Schools in School Board Districts." 1893.
11. Church Committee for Church Defence and Church Instruction:
    I. *The Church and Education prior to 1870.* Feb., 1898.
    II. *The Church and Education since 1870.* Dec., 1903.
12. The Manuscript Minute Books of the Society, esp. 1833–9.

For the Secondary Schools

1. Bp. K. E. Kirk: *The Story of the Woodard Schools.* 1937.
2. *The Public Schools' Year Book.* Annually.
3. Canon J. L. Brereton: *County Education.* 1861.
4. *Report of the Royal Commission on Secondary Education.* (Bryce.) 1895.
5. *Secondary Education.* (Spens Report.) 1938. pp. 1–86.
6. *National Society Middle Class School Committee.* Report, Class Lists, and Examination Papers for 1871. 1872.
7. Ed. by Acland and Llewellyn Smith: *Studies in Secondary Education.* 1892.
8. *Report of the Schools Inquiry Commission.* (Taunton.) 1868.
9. The Schools Sections of the various volumes in the *Victoria County History* of different counties are often helpful.
10. R. L. Archer: *Secondary Education in the Nineteenth Century.* 1921.

For the Church Training Colleges

1. M. Graham Brown: *Training in Truro—1813–1938.* 1938.
2. Ed. Rev. G. W. Gent: *Memorials of St. Mark's College.* 1891.
3. Rev. Derwent Coleridge: "A Letter on the National Society's Training College for Schoolmasters."
4.   do.   : "The Teachers of the People, a Tract for the Times." 1862.
5. *Year Books of St. Mark's College.*
6. G. Ashley Wood: *History of Hockerill Training College.* 1938.

7. " Training College Commission. Report to the Archbishop of Canterbury. Nov., 1916."
8. Thomas Adkins: *History of St. John's College, Battersea.* 1906.
9. " Report of the Committee of Inquiry presented to the Board of Supervision of the Church's Training Colleges." 1933.

INDEX

PRINTED IN GREAT BRITAIN BY THE FAITH PRESS, LTD., LEIGHTON BUZZARD